Drive and Stroll in

Cumbria and the Lake District

Chris Bagshaw

D1147559

COUNTRYSIDE BOOKS
NEWBURY BERKSHIRE

COUNTRYSIDE BOOKS
3 Catherine Road
Newbury, Berkshire

To view our complete range of books,
please visit us at
www.countrysidebooks.co.uk

ISBN 978 1 84674 075 6

Produced through MRM Associates Ltd., Reading
Typeset by Mac Style, Nafferton, East Yorkshire
Printed by Information Press, Oxford

All material for the manufacture of this book
was sourced from sustainable forests.

Contents

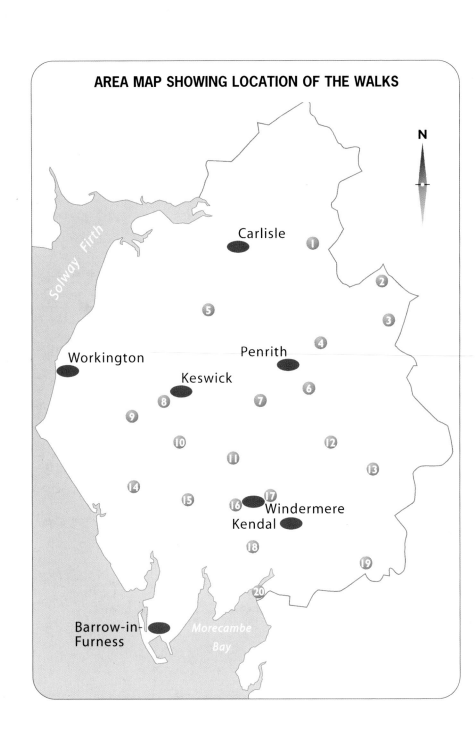

Contents ❧

PUBLISHER'S NOTE

We hope that you obtain considerable enjoyment from this book; great care has been taken in its preparation. Although at the time of publication all routes followed public rights of way or permitted paths, diversion orders can be made and permissions withdrawn.

We cannot, of course, be held responsible for such diversion orders and any inaccuracies in the text which result from these or any other changes to the routes nor any damage which might result from walkers trespassing on private property. We are anxious though that all details covering the walks are kept up to date and would therefore welcome information from readers which would be relevant to future editions.

The simple sketch maps that accompany the walks in this book are based on notes made by the author whilst checking out the routes on the ground. They are designed to show you how to reach the start, to point out the main features of the overall circuit and they contain a progression of numbers that relate to the paragraphs of the text.

However, for the benefit of a proper map, we do recommend that you purchase the relevant Ordnance Survey sheet covering your walk. The Ordnance Survey maps are widely available, especially through booksellers and local newsagents.

Introduction ❧

Somebody asked me if I ever got bored with walking in the Lake District. I mulled the suggestion over for a while – I've been expending Vibram soles here since I was 8 years old. I thought of the oft-visited summits of Great Gable and Blencathra, Helvellyn and High Street and began to waiver. Then I thought about primroses on the banks of the River Esk, the fixed chains around the corner of Johnny Wood in Borrowdale, the spooky wooded heights of Claife above the Windermere ferry and the always serene shores of Grasmere. Of course I never get bored when there is so much to see at all levels. There are those who may tell you that you have to climb a fell to enjoy this landscape. Well there are 20 reasons in this book why that isn't the case. You can savour the woods of Brandlehow, overlooking Derwent Water, linger on the shore of Buttermere, even when the cloud is down to 200 ft, or even join the gaze of Alfred Wainwright himself from Orrest Head's modest eminence. But there is a bigger picture to be seen.

This book steps out of the straitjacket imposed by the Lake District National Park boundary, exploring the wider administrative area known as Cumbria. For some it is an artificial creation – a heterogeneous amalgam of Cumberland, Westmorland, a bit of Lancashire that was stranded across Morecambe Bay and a corner of the West Riding of Yorkshire, where the rivers have always treacherously flowed into the Lune instead of the Ouse. But for me it is a natural geographical unit, a peninsula of intricate hills, bounded on all sides by sea and more hills.

In the east, the Pennines rise to their highest point and we can experience that wild beauty from the very head of the South Tyne Valley. Alston Moor was once the lead mining capital of the world, but now is a fascinating upland community, a million miles from the bustle of commuterland or the noise of through traffic. The accents may be distinctive here, but the boundaries have stayed resolutely to the east of this moorland enclave for many hundreds of years. Over the Pennine edge to the west is what Eden Valley folk refer to as the East Fellside. Complex geological processes created this wall of mountain, but it was the movement of ice over its northern tip that created lovely Talkin Tarn. This is Carlisle's secret lake, a glacial contrivance hidden by green ridges, just a few miles to the east of the border city. It's as far north as this collection goes; I had to make some hard choices and the harsh landscape north of Hadrian's Wall lost out to more accessible gems further south. One of these gems was Lady's Walk, a delightful stretch of the River Eden near Langwathby, created for the strolling ladies of nearby Edenhall. Another was the fabulous railway track through the nature reserve at Smardale. There is so much archaeology and history going on here that it is difficult for a non-naturalist like me to appreciate that this landscape is

actually preserved for its important living environment. Over the limestone fells from Smardale lies the valley of the Lyvennet Beck, where you can easily believe that the warrior king Urien of Rheged, the last great British kingdom in England, built his palace. These Westmorland dales may be about to join with their Yorkshire neighbours in an extended national park, or they may get their own protective designation as an Area of Outstanding Natural Beauty. Whatever becomes of them, you would hope they get the preservation and recognition they richly deserve.

One part of Cumbria outside the Lake District already has this status. Dentdale, along with Sedbergh and Garsdale, is an important north-westerly outpost of the Yorkshire Dales National Park. Following the Dales Way along Deepdale Beck or through the spring-line farmyards that line the foot of the fell, you may realise that these Cumbrians have no doubt about their Yorkshire heritage.

The most southerly walk in the book is also the least like any of the others. Arnside Knott juts out into the sandy mass of Morecambe Bay like a limestone knuckle. The shoreline path from Far Arnside, round the headlands back into the village is a fine seaside experience, even when the vast tide has rendered the actual sea to be several miles away.

So these are lovely walks, all circular, seldom physically challenging, but occasionally demanding a bit more effort than merely stepping out of the car. That effort is rewarded by the knowledge that you have found a fascinating, quiet landscape usually away from the tourist hordes and certainly never boring.

Chris Bagshaw

1 Talkin Tarn

The northern shore of Talkin Tarn

Distance 1³/₄ miles 🕐 1¹/₂ hours
Map: OS Explorer 315 (GR 543590)

How to get there

The B6413 runs from the A69 at Brampton to the A6 at Plumpton, just north of Penrith. Talkin Tarn is at the northern end of this road, a couple of miles out of Brampton. There's a signposted access road about 200 yards south of the railway crossing. **Parking:** A large car park is situated at the northern edge of the tarn; disc parking for the first two hours, after which it's pay-and-display.

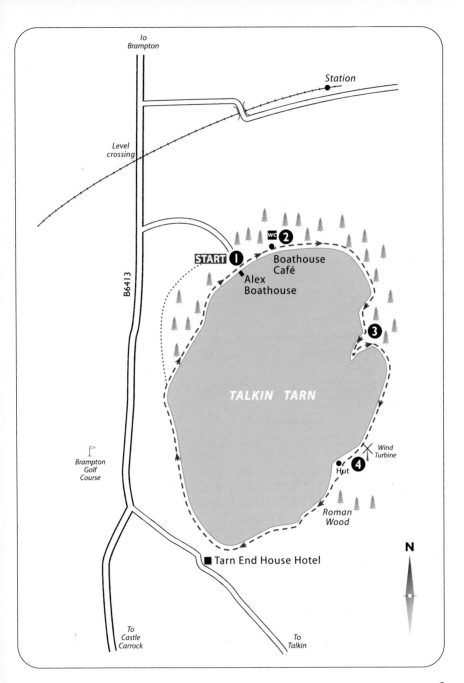

9

Drive and Stroll

Introduction

For those in the know, this is one of Cumbria's most popular lakes, but it's not in the Lake District. The 65-acre tarn was formed at the foot of the North Pennines by an ice sheet moving eastwards into the Tyne Gap as far back as 18,000 years ago. Surrounded by a ring of drumlins (mounds of glacial debris), it is fed by underground streams. It's been popular with the locals since at least the 1850s, when regular rowing regattas began, and has been a country park since 1976. Its circuit is easy and level, but the changing light and colours through the seasons brings people back time after time.

The Boathouse Café

Sitting back from the tarn in a prominent position above the boat launching area, the Boathouse Café has a terrace for summer evenings and a roaring log fire for bitter winter afternoons. Food is mostly on the light side, with a range of mezzalunas (herby paninis), jacket potatoes and salads, as well as hot soup and home-made cakes. There is a licence, so you can enjoy a cold beer on a hot day or a soothing glass of wine. Telephone: 01697 741050.

THE WALK

From the car park, take the right-hand exit down to the lake, joining the circular path by the **Alexander boathouse**. You can walk either way around the tarn but I think you avoid the coldest winds (when necessary) if you go clockwise. So turn left and go along the shoreline towards the **Boathouse Café** and the main buildings of the country park.

In summer this is the boating area – you can hire rowing boats and people launch their sailing dinghies. The rowing club here is one of the oldest in the country – it was formed in 1859 – and still holds annual regattas. The club building is behind the café, next to the Ranger Centre.

The path continues past some interesting willow structures and a wooden dog, poised to pounce on an invisible stick.

Much of the stand of trees you can see across the little bay to your right is actually on an island. Many of the trees around the lake are non-native to the north of England. Here there are Scots pine and Western hemlock, elsewhere you'll find beech is dominant.

The Alexander boathouse

↳ ③

A deviation from the path on the right brings the island a little closer, but the island itself is now off-limits to visitors – it is a valuable nesting site and the conservation value outweighed the needs of children in wellies. From the barrier at the end of the little peninsula, return to the main track and turn right to continue your circuit. The lakeshore now opens out. Ignore a turning on your left to **Farlam village** and carry on towards the wind turbine.

The old boathouse here has been turned into a bird observatory, with a window opening out onto the water. The tarn has suffered greatly in the past from green algae. It's poisonous to livestock, so all the grassland had to be fenced off from the water's edge. Now an artificial aeration system has been introduced and the problem is slowly dissipating.

↳ ④

The path continues past the **Roman Wood** to **Tarn End**. Here you dip briefly into the gardens of the **Tarn End House Hotel**, before swinging back round for the final quarter mile to the car park.

Before you reach the boathouse, as you pass the elaborate weaving of the Willow Hide, the path is plunged into a shady beechwood for the last 100 yards. Rabbits have made most of the holes in the bank here, but there are many other, more shy creatures lurking around the tarn. The Alex boathouse has been home to an otter; red squirrels, roe deer and badgers are frequent visitors to the woodland, while tawny owls and buzzards quarter the skies above.

Turn left for your car or keep straight on for the café and toilets.

2 | Alston and Blagill

Gossipgate Waterfall on the River Nent

Distance 3¹/₂ miles 🕐 2 hours
Map: OS Explorer OL31 (GR 716467)

How to get there

Alston is 20 miles from Penrith, on the A686 north of the Hartside Pass. From the A69, it's 18 miles south of Haydon Bridge (also on the A686) or 18 miles from Brampton on the A689. **Parking:** There is a free car park over the level crossing by the station, signposted from the north of town off the A686.

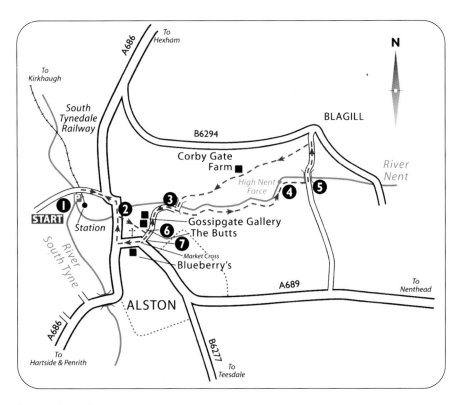

Introduction

Alston is a small town, high up in the North Pennines. A quirk of medieval mineral rights put it in the county of Cumberland, though its main river is the South Tyne and the district is surrounded on three sides by Northumberland and Durham. A boom time for the local lead mines in the mid 19th century saw the parish's population soar to nearly 7,000, but now it is barely 2,000. You'll see plenty of evidence of the industrial times on this walk, from mine tailings at Blagill to the old foundry site at the bottom end of the town.

Blueberry's

This snug little teashop sits in the bottom corner of Alston's old market square. Inside, beneath the beams and in front of a fire in winter, you'll find refreshingly different hot sandwich fillings such as goat's cheese and sun-dried tomatoes or black pudding and bacon. There's a huge all-day breakfast, with a veggie version too, as well as soup, cream teas and a tempting board of desserts. Telephone: 01434 381928.

THE WALK

①

From the station car park, cross the railway by the level crossing and turn right. Walk up the road and turn right again, along the pavement at the top.

The South Tynedale Railway is a narrow-gauge line from Alston to Kirkhaugh, $2^1/_4$ miles away. It opened in 1983 on the trackbed of the old Alston–Haltwhistle branch railway, which was closed by British Rail in 1976. Opposite the main road junction is the site of the Alston Foundry. This was once a major employer in the town, but it closed in 1980.

 ②

In 50 yards cross the road to a path between buildings, signposted to **Gossipgate Gallery**. A flight of steps leads up into an area known as **The Butts**. When you reach a junction by **Rasper House**, turn left past the gallery and down a lane to the **River Nent**.

The Butts is one of the oldest parts of town, taking its name from the medieval archery practice area. The gallery was formerly a Congregational chapel.

 ③

At the bridge, cross the stile on your right and continue on the riverside path through a field. Another stile leads into woodland and the path now continues up the valley.

The geology of Alston Moor fills several volumes in its own right. Here the rock is several different beds of limestone and sandstone. The waterfall has eaten away at the bedrock, causing the little gorges to form. Further upstream this process is seen more dramatically at High Nent Force.

 ④

In $^3/_4$ mile the path bends round to the left with the river and climbs the bank to emerge, beyond a stile, at the head of **High Nent Force**. Continue upstream through meadowland to a gate onto a surfaced road.

The mine workings you can see here have their origins in the 14th century, but Blagill became famous in the 19th century, not for lead, but for a mineral called barytocalcite, which was unique to this little side valley.

Market Cross, Alston

⑤

Turn left along the road, crossing the bridge and climbing up to the hamlet of **Blagill**. A bridleway sign points you left, past a barn and through a gate into a field. Follow the edge of the field through a series of gates to the edge of a garden. Marker posts lead you through several gates to emerge on an enclosed track. Turn left and continue to follow the marker posts down across several fields to join another enclosed track. This takes you all the way down to the bridge you passed earlier. Cross the bridge and turn right to retrace your footsteps back to **The Butts**.

 ⑥

At **Rasper House** this time, though, carry straight on, walking up into the centre of town by the market cross and the **Turks Head**.

The market cross was originally built by a local man, Sir William Stephenson, in 1765, shortly after he became Lord Mayor of London. Most of the buildings around the steep main street date from the 17th and 18th centuries, making this a popular shooting location for period dramas. As you pass the church gates, going down the hill, you'll see the crest of the Greenwich Hospital. The mineral rights in the parish were granted to the hospital trustees after Lord Derwentwater's lands were confiscated for his support of the Jacobite rebellion of 1715.

 ⑦

After spending a little time looking at the interesting shops, descend the main street, past the **Angel Inn** and the town hall to a T-junction at the bottom. Turn right here to return to the station car park.

3

At the top of the South Tyne

The River South Tyne

Distance $3^1/_2$ miles ⏱ 2 hours
Map: OS Explorer OL31 (GR 757383)

How to get there

From the Penrith direction, turn eastwards off the A686 about 3 miles east of the Hartside Café, signposted to Leadgate and Garrigill. Turn right at the next junction and follow the road to Garrigill. Alternatively, drive south from Alston on the B6277, turning off right to Garrigill. Go through the village, past the church on the left. Keep on this road now for another 2 miles, until, over a cattle grid, it becomes a rough track. **Parking:** There is space to park considerably on the verge, just over the cattle grid.

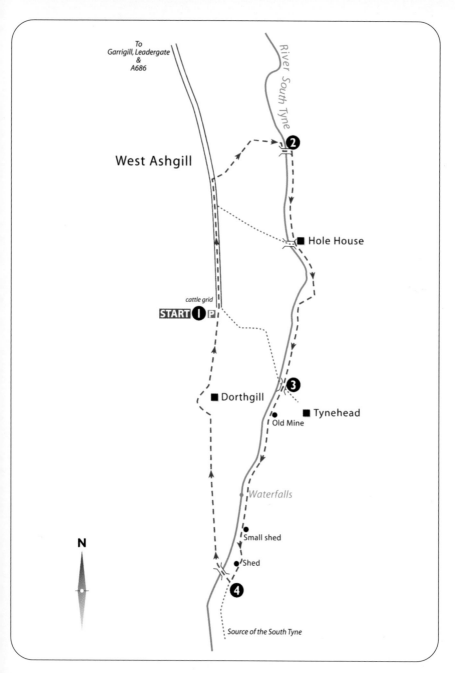

To
Garrigill, Leadergate
&
A686

River South Tyne

West Ashgill

2

■ Hole House

cattle grid

START **1** P

3

■ Dorthgill

■ Tynehead

● Old Mine

Waterfalls

● Small shed

● Shed

4

Source of the South Tyne

N

Drive and Stroll

Introduction

The upper reaches of the South Tyne are as unlike any other part of Cumbria as central Whitehaven and the summit of Scafell. Here is a remote dales landscape, hardly touched by tourists, where the cry of the curlew and peewit is the loudest and where you feel even the ubiquitous lead miners of old struggled to make any lasting mark on this huge canvas of high moorland. The river is often hidden from view in a tiny gorge, occasionally letting you glimpse a waterfall or two amidst meadows rich in flowers and grasses. The paths are well signed but not so well trodden, so some care will be needed underfoot.

The George and Dragon Inn

Overlooking Garrigill's wide green, the George and Dragon is a worthy hub of the local community and an important waymark on the Pennine Way, which passes its door after the long descent from nearby Cross Fell. As well as a good selection of real ales and locally sourced beef, seasonal vegetables and sausage, they do a nifty line in Asian and African dishes, or you can call in just for chips. Telephone: 01434 381293.

THE WALK

Walk back over the cattle grid and along the road for about 500 yards, towards a house on the right. Before you get there, a fingerpost points you over a stile into the field. Head diagonally left towards the field boundary, and follow this down to the river. Turn right along the riverbank to a bridge over the **South Tyne**.

Cross the bridge and stile, then turn right, picking up a faint path, aiming for a stile.

You've now joined the South Tyne Trail and you stay with this for the next couple of miles. Much of the path is along the edge of meadowland that is rich in diversity. Relatively unscarred by agricultural changes since the Second World War, over 40% of England's remaining hay meadows are in the North Pennines.

Cross the stile and continue ahead, with the river on your right, on the indistinct grassy path, heading for some farm buildings. Follow the markers around the farm buildings and continue on a track, veering away from the river. Over a stile bear right with a wall. Just before the river, the path swings left along the bank. Fingerposts now guide

Remote Tynehead House

you by meadow edges to a gated stile onto a track at **Tynehead**.

This settlement is now largely deserted but at the height of the lead mining boom in the mid 19th century, there were enough families living here to support a school.

Cross the footbridge over the **Clargill Burn** and turn left through a gate, continuing up the valley. Fingerposts guide you through old mine workings and the path crosses a beck to join a terraced path.

This is the site of the Sir John's mine and smelter. The lead ore was particularly rich in silver here. Rumours of gold in the 19th century caused a flurry of prospecting, but they proved to be ill-founded.

Stay with the riverside path over a stile and continue, now on a permissive path, towards a stand of pines ahead. Cross several more stiles and pass a pair of waterfalls. Beyond a tin shed, turn left, then right with a sign, heading for a larger building. Marker posts lead you over several streams to a fingerpost on a surfaced track.

The waterfalls are caused by an intrusion of the volcanic Whin Sill into the softer local carboniferous rocks. The Great Sulphur Vein, which is where the miners found their lead, can be glimpsed as a line of shimmering quartz, at the top of one of the lower falls just above the mine.

You can follow this road all the way to the actual source of the South Tyne from here, another mile or so upstream, and the bridleway continues to the extreme remoteness of Moor House.

This is the centre of a vast National Nature Reserve that stretches for $28\frac{1}{2}$ square miles from the summit of Cross Fell down to High Force in Teesdale. It is England's largest and highest nature reserve, its blanket bogs and peatland forming a complete drainage system of international importance.

Cross the bridge to the right and follow the road, passing the ruins of **Dorthgill farmhouse** before reaching your car.

4 Langwathby, Edenhall and Lady's Walk

Looking across the green at Langwathby

Distance 3½ miles 🕐 2 hours
Map: OS Explorer OL5 (GR 569336)

How to get there

Langwathby is 4 miles east of Penrith, on the A686. **Parking:** There is parking available around the village green in Langwathby and adjacent to the Shepherds Inn.

Drive and Stroll

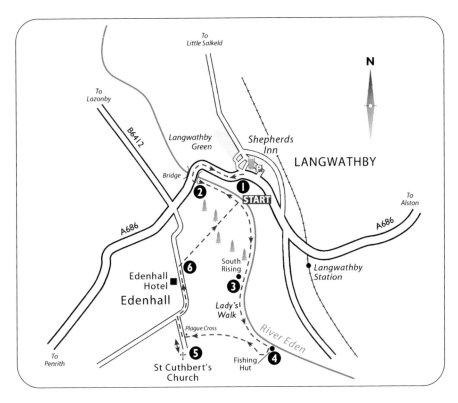

Introduction
The central section of this easy walk takes its name from the promenade built by the Musgrave family of Edenhall, a gentle stretch of riverside path where the ladies of the house could enjoy the views across the water to the high fells of the North Pennines beyond. The river is usually placid but in flood it has a more violent side. In 1968 it washed away the magnificent old bridge that connected the two villages of Edenhall and Langwathby. Since then the main road has used a temporary Bailey bridge, controlled by traffic lights. It's now reputed to be the longest serving temporary bridge in Britain.

The Shepherds Inn
On the centre of the green in Langwathby, the Shepherds serves a wide range of food from light snacks and filled baguettes, to full-on main meals of steak pie, fish or vegetarian options such as herb and suet roulade and spinach and ricotta cannelloni. There are usually a couple of real ales, often including one from the Hesket Newmarket Brewery. Telephone: 01768 881335.

THE WALK

From the **Shepherds Inn**, walk over to the main road and bear right, down the road towards the bridge and the river. Cross the bridge on the pedestrian walkway, then go over the road to a kissing gate on the other side.

Look under the bridge and you can see the sandstone parapets of the old bridge. If you haven't seen the Eden in full flood here, the size of this structure and its height above the usual water level is a good indicator of how epic it can be.

Now follow the riverside path. In 400 yards, ignore the path off to the right and continue, veering round to the right and through a kissing gate by the trees. Beyond this the path rises up the bank to a sandstone sculpture.

'South Rising' by Vivien Monsdell is one of ten sculptures in the Millennium project known as Eden Benchmarks. They occupy significant sections of the river's story, from the heights of Mallerstang to the marshes at Rockcliffe.

Beyond this the path dips again, down steps to join a balcony path alongside the river.

This is the Lady's Walk proper. The retaining wall was constructed in 1870 by Lady Musgrave, using stone from the churchyard.

In front of a fishing hut, bear right, through a gate, then sharp right up the track and across the field to a gate by the stone cross. Turn left here to visit **St Cuthbert's church**.

The Plague Cross stands on a plinth rediscovered when the church wall was excavated for Lady's Walk. Its bowl would have held vinegar to disinfect money left to pay for food, probably during a typhus outbreak in the 16th century, to which a quarter of the village's population succumbed. St Cuthbert's church has 12th-century foundations. It was fortified in the 15th century then heavily 'restored' in 1834.

From the church, retrace your steps past the cross and continue along the lane into the village of **Edenhall**. Bear right, along the road past the hotel.

Looking across the Eden to Cross Fell from Edenhall

The Musgrave family occupied Edenhall from medieval times. They are famously associated with a glass cup known as the Luck of Edenhall. Probably originating in Syria and brought to England after the Crusades, the cup was reputedly lost by fairies near St Cuthbert's Well. Disturbed by a family retainer they fled, leaving the cup behind them, but yelling the curse: 'If e'er this cup shall break or fall, farewell the Luck of Edenhall!' The Musgraves' luck ran out in 1934 when debts forced the sale of the estate and the demolition of their Victorian mansion. The cup is now in the Victoria and Albert Museum.

 ⑥

Just beyond a children's play area on the right, locate a kissing gate and follow the field-edge path down into a gap into the shelter belt. Beyond this you rejoin your outward route, over the bridge back into **Langwathby**.

5 | Hesket Newmarket and Caldbeck

Priest's Mill, Caldbeck

Distance 4½ miles ⏰ 2 hours
Map: OS Explorer OL5 (GR 342386)

How to get there

Hesket Newmarket is on the very north-eastern tip of the Lake District National Park, 15 miles north-west of Penrith. From junction 41 of the M6 follow the B5305 north for about 10 miles. A left turn is prominently signposted to Hesket Newmarket and Caldbeck. Follow this road into the centre of the village. **Parking:** There is a National Park Authority car park (free) on the eastern side of the village, opposite the junction of the Carlisle and Penrith roads.

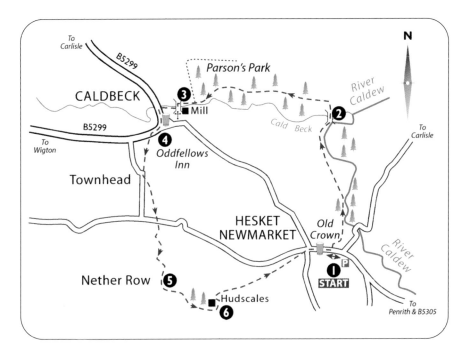

Introduction

Hesket Newmarket and Caldbeck can justifiably claim to be two of Lakeland's hidden gems. The villages are a couple of miles apart and whilst the former has become famous for its excellent little cooperatively-run pub and brewery, much loved by Prince Charles, the latter boasts an impressive parish church and mill, cafés and a riverside walk. The 'new market' was founded on Hesket's village green in the 18th century, but it wasn't a great success; today this is a relatively rare example of a planned village within the National Park. This walk takes in woodlands and riverside outside the park boundary, before heading up towards the hill country 'Back o' Skidda' to return.

The Old Crown

Oft-frequented by the Prince of Wales on his visits to the area, the Old Crown has become a byword for sustainable rural pubs. Owned by a cooperative of villagers, and serving the excellent Hesket Newmarket beers produced by the (also cooperatively-run) brewery at the rear, the feel good factor is fully justified. For food the emphasis is on local produce so expect to find plenty of locally-reared beef and lamb, as well as hot sandwiches, soup and the inevitable Cumberland sausage. Telephone: 01697 478288.

THE WALK

From the car park cross the green to a kissing gate, opposite the pub. Follow the track across a field then through another gate and right. An obvious path marked by yellow arrows continues through trees, eventually reaching the bank of the **River Caldew** at a dramatic bend in the river. The well-marked path continues, leaving the riverbank again to cut across a field, before rejoining it in more steep woodland. Emerging briefly, descend to a gate into woods and a bridge on the left.

The River Caldew rises on the high flanks of Skiddaw and flows due east before geology funnels it into a northerly course around the foot of the fells. Once it has met with the Cald Beck, it steers away from the hill country altogether, passing through Dalston and Cummersdale before reaching Carlisle. It joins the Eden just beyond Bitts Park.

Cross the bridge and ascend the path going straight ahead on the other side. Crossing an open area it then climbs up steeply to join a track coming in from the right. Turn left and follow this muddy bridleway. At a junction bear left, dropping down to the riverside. Now follow the river past the water treatment works and into **Caldbeck** village.

The mill here was built to grind corn by the rector of the nearby church in 1702. It continued milling until 1933 when it became a sawmill. In 1965 a flood damaged the water supply and it was a ruin until restoration in 1986. It now houses a café and craft shops.

At the first bridge turn left across the beck, then go right above **St Kentigern's Well** and follow the tiny riverside path to the road. Cross over and turn left, keeping right at the junction to pass the **Old Forge Tearoom**.

St Kentigern's Well stands behind St Kentigern's church, taking their name from a man elsewhere known as St. Mungo. He was a 6th-century Brythonic religious leader who established a cathedral in Glasgow and was also active in Cumbria and Wales. In the churchyard you can see the grave of John Peel, the notorious huntsman immortalised in song, and Mary Robinson who, as a teenager in the 1790s, was far-famed as the Maid of Buttermere.

At the top, turn right and cross the bridge by the toilets. Walk in front

Hesket Newmarket's green and market cross

of a row of cottages. Beyond them, turn left and join an enclosed track. Beyond a gate, stay with the path over a footbridge and up to a gate. In the field beyond, walk ahead beneath the transmission poles to a gate onto an access road. Turn right, down the road, then left, and immediately left again between width restriction signs. Continue up the narrow lane to a crossroads and carry straight on; the lane is signposted 'Nether Row and Potts Gill'. Follow it round a series of bends to reach the hamlet of **Nether Row**.

Caldbeck's history is tightly enmeshed with that of the mines that developed here on the fellside. An old saying went 'Caldbeck and the Caldbeck Fells are worth all England else'. They were mined for lead from the 12th century, and the Elizabethans were very active. There was a boom in the 19th century and the 20th century saw several operations come and go. Potts Gill had an ancient copper mine and two very productive barytes mines. Mining ceased with the closure of nearby Sandbeds mine in 1966, though there was still work over the fell at Carrock Wolfram Mine as late as 1981.

 ⑤

At **Nether Row**, as the lane swings to the left, pick out the middle track ahead, to the left of a house. A path leads off to the left over a wall into a rough field. Follow the field boundary on the right, up to a gap. Cross over, then continue following the wall, round the top of the field, finally crossing it to a ladder stile onto the open fell, near the end of a stand of trees. Turn left for 250 yards until a gap in the trees allows you to follow a permissive path left to **Hudscales**.

⑥

Turn left through the farmyard and descend the access track to a bend. Leave the track here for a field path on the right, following the right-hand side of the wall ahead. Descend now through six fields, mostly keeping to the right after the second one, to emerge in **Hesket Newmarket** at a flight of steps. Turn right to return to the green and your car.

6 Askham and Moor Divock

Distance 6$^1/_2$ miles 🕐 3$^1/_2$ hours
Map: OS Explorer OL5 (GR 506234)

How to get there

From Penrith, head south on the A6 to Eamont Bridge. Turn right on the B5320 and in a mile or so there is a left turn, by Yanwath School, for Askham. In the village, turn right, up the past the higher green, to reach the fell edge. **Parking:** Ample parking on the verge and around the edge of the fell at the road end.

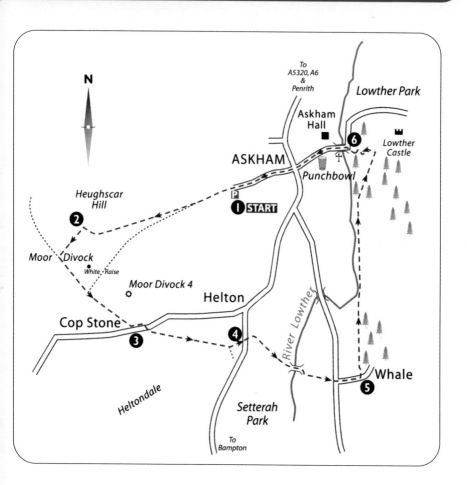

Introduction

This is quite a long walk, but the diversity of landscape it covers makes it well worthwhile. The fell above Askham is dotted with traces of a prehistoric culture. There are stone circles, standing stones, tumuli, and even a Roman road. The view up the Ullswater valley from the ridge of Heughscar Hill is worth the effort alone. The second part of the walk is in the valley of the River Lowther – a place as dominated by one family as the name suggests. Here is a fine deer park (transformed during the annual Lowther horse trials), the ruins of a huge gothic mansion and views up to the Shap Fells that will surprise and impress anyone unfamiliar with this less-frequented corner of the Lake District National Park.

Drive and Stroll

The Punchbowl
Of the two pubs in Askham, the Punchbowl is the more adventurous with its food. As you'd expect at the heart of the Lowther Estate, there's a fair smattering of local game – pheasant breast, partridge – and organic chicken, as well as fell-bred lamb and Cumbrian beef. For vegetarians there's a hot vegetable meze or a vegetable paella, and the specials board is usually extensive. Telephone: 01931 712443.

THE WALK

Beyond the cattle grid, walk straight ahead up the track, keeping the wall on your right. Where the track veers left, go straight on up a grassy slope to a gate in the wall ahead. On the moorland beyond, bear right, continuing up the slope towards a line of trees on the horizon. At the brow of the hill, keep right for 200 yards to get a view of **Ullswater**.

The marshy terrain in front of you is called Moor Divock. It is probably the most accessible of Cumbria's prehistoric landscapes, with dozens of lumps, bumps, stones and carvings dating back to the earliest times. The most notable are the White Raise burial cairn, due south from your position, and the Cockpit stone circle, a little further to the south-west. A recent survey added 44 new sites to the archaeological record and showed that many were placed around a small tarn, which has long since vanished.

Now pick one of the tracks down the slope in front of you, heading for a prominent crossing track, running north-west to south-east, about 500 yards due north of the ridge. Turn left along the track. In another 500 yards or so, you'll see a stone circle in the bracken and bog to your left.

The circle is somewhat prosaically known as Moor Divock 4.

Continue past a solitary standing stone to reach a road.

This is the Cop Stone, a glacial erratic that may or may not have some ritual significance, depending on what you believe.

Turn left for about 75 yards before turning right, down the slope with a fingerpost to **Setterah Park**. Go down to a gate and stile. Beyond this the path descends a long field diagonally to the bottom left corner.

On the route

A gate and stile lead into a narrow field. At the bottom right corner of this a gate leads to an enclosed lane. After a few yards look for a little gate on the left. Through this, head diagonally across the field to a gap in the bottom left-hand corner, between the hedge and a gate. Over a stile, drop down into the next field, looking for a stile halfway down the far side. A gate at the other side of the next field leads to steps and the road.

This is the edge of Helton village, sadly no longer served by a pub, but still worthy of a few minutes' wandering.

☟ ④

Turn left for a few paces, then right between buildings to drop down to the main road. Cross over and go straight ahead down the bridleway towards **Whale**. The enclosed track leads to a meadow by a bridge over the **Lowther**. Cross the bridge and turn right through a gate. Turn immediately left, through another gate and ascend the grassy track to meet a road. Cross over and maintain your direction up into **Whale**.

The flow of the River Lowther is controlled by a dam at Wet Sleddale. It is rich in trout and is also an important spawning ground for salmon.

☟ ⑤

At the far side of **Penfold Cottage**, turn left along a footpath, passing a gate and stile into a field. Head for a kissing gate on the right, onto a track. The right of way here disappears into the wood. You may find it easier to turn left along the estate track, which leaves the woodland by a gate and rejoins the right of way at another gate by the river. Follow this good track now through the deer park and into the woods beyond. At a junction veer right, up the slope to the edge of the **Lowther Castle** garden wall.

You can peek round the corner here, not only at the most elaborate garden gate you'll ever see but also at the ruins of the castle itself. The Lowthers can trace their ancestry back to the 12th century and were prominent local knights throughout the Middle Ages. Their real power came with William III's 'glorious revolution' in 1688. Sir John Lowther was William's Lord Privy Seal and was promoted to Viscount Lonsdale. By the time James Lowther inherited from three separate branches of the family, there were slaving interests in the West Indies and America, and involvement in Whitehaven's coal mines to add to the fortune. The castle was built for the, by now, Earl of Lowther between in 1806 and 1813. It was abandoned as a house in 1937 and it has been roofless since 1957.

From the wall corner, a steep track zig-zags down towards the river, emerging by a bridge.

☟ ⑥

Cross the river and walk up the road, back into the village. Pass the lower green, cross the main road and pass the higher green to get back to your car on the fell edge.

7 Sandwick Bay and Ullswater

On the road to 'Sannick'

Distance 4 miles 🕐 2 hours
Map: OS Explorer OL5 (GR 439194)

How to get there

From junction 40 on the M6, take the A66 towards Keswick then the A592 at the Rheged roundabout. At the next T-junction, by Ullswater, turn left into Pooley Bridge. Drive through the village and turn right by the village hall. Turn right again, following the minor road for 4 miles to Howtown. **Parking:** Pass the steamer pier and the hotel to find a parking space on the roadside at the foot of the zigzags that lead up to Martindale Hause. Please park considerately and don't block any passing places.

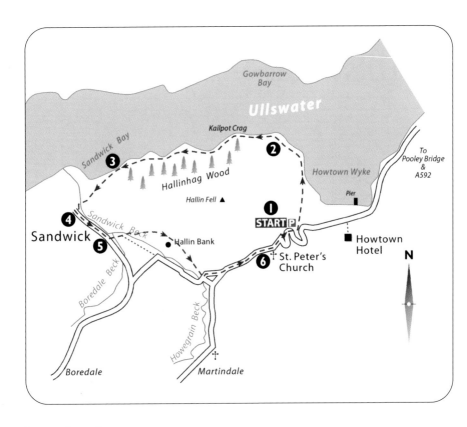

Introduction
Ullswater is one of the big four lakes of the National Park, with Windermere, Coniston Water and Derwent Water. This walk takes you along its remote southern shore, through magnificent woodlands to emerge at the hamlet of Sandwick, as far from a main road as you can get without catching a boat! The return is around the southern flanks of Hallin Fell, dipping into the idyllic valleys of Boredale and Martindale.

The Sun Inn, Pooley Bridge
The nearest spot for refreshments is the Howtown Hotel, but its opening is seasonal, so you may have to schlep back into Pooley Bridge if you're after a pint or a cup of tea. Pick of the bunch here is the Sun Inn, a busy Jennings pub with a large garden to cater for the summer hordes. As well as a changing specials board, you can rely on Waberthwaite sausage or braised lamb Jennings, or check out the five-bean hot pot. Telephone: 01768 486205.

THE WALK

From the parking area, with your back to the road, turn right, to pick up a prominent footpath, signposted to Sandwick and Patterdale. The path contours around the foot of the open fell towards the lake. Ignore paths joining from left and right, continuing ahead until it laps at the foot of the slope below you.

Ullswater is the second largest of the Cumbrian lakes. It's 9 miles long and ¾ mile wide at its broadest. A legacy of the glaciers that retreated from here over 10,000 years ago, the deepest parts are over 200 ft deep.

Here you leave the shelter of **Howtown Wyke**. A rocky promontory affords fine views across the lake. The path descends now on rocky steps to just a few feet above the shore, before rising again through a gate leading into woodland. Here, another craggy outcrop jutting into the lake offers excitement for children and anxiety for parents. The path stays well back from the edge and continues through the woods. Sometimes it is a little rough and rocky but the way is always clear.

Pressure to develop the lake and its shore has been high since Victorian times. Gowbarrow Park, on the opposite shore, was an early purchase of the National Trust and as late as the 1960s there were plans to raise the lake's level to supply water to urban Lancashire. The 'steamers' (they've been diesel since the 1930s) began plying the lake in the 1850s, originally carrying slate and lead from the workings at the head of the valley.

After about ¾ mile or so, the sweep of grass in **Sandwick Bay** comes into view and the woodland track emerges through a kissing gate onto a causeway above the sandy beach. Beyond this first short bay the path rises again through a series of fields and gates, leading eventually to **Sandwick Beck**. Here it swings left, then right to cross the bridge into this remote hamlet.

Beckside Farm was bought by the National Park in the 1960s to protect and conserve its character. It was sold again to a private buyer as a going concern in 2007.

On the far side of the bridge, go through the gate and walk up the road.

Drive and Stroll

A real Postman Pat, testing the hairnins to... *(rotated caption, partially legible)*

↳ ⑤

In ¹⁄₄ mile turn left and cross a bridge. Walk on up the lane to a pair of gates. Take the right-hand one leading over a wooden bridge. Over the bridge turn right, through a wicket gate and stile to join a riverside path to a gate. Beyond this a well-defined grassy path leads up a field to a white house, halfway up the hillside. Here a gate leads to the access road behind the former farm buildings. Beyond the garages, pass through another gate and descend on the track running parallel with the beck below. When you reach a junction with a surfaced road, by a bridge, turn left up the steep road, passing several buildings before levelling out at the top of the hause by **St Peter's church**.

This is the dale's new church, being completed in 1882. It contains some striking stained glass from the 1970s. The dale's old church, St Martin's, is about a mile away, back in the valley behind you. It can trace its foundation to the 13th century, but it was collapsing when a local benefactor offered to pay for a new one. It's said that the old roof finally collapsed on the day the new church was dedicated. It has since been restored and is a good example of a simple 17th-century Lakeland chapel.

↳ ⑥

Continue on the road over the hause, descending the zigzags to return to your car.

8 | Brandlehow and Derwent Water

Brandlehow Point, Derwent Water

Distance 4¹/₂ miles 🕐 2¹/₂ hours
Map: OS Explorer OL4 (GR 247212). Please note that Brandlehow is confusingly spelt 'Brandelhow' on the OS map.

How to get there

From the A66 Keswick bypass, take the turn off to Portinscale. Drive through the village then through the woods, keeping left at two junctions. After 2¹/₂ miles you will reach Hawes End. **Parking:** There is roadside parking in the trees around the steep bend before the cattle grid. Ensure you don't block a field entry and leave enough space for a bus to pass.

Drive and Stroll

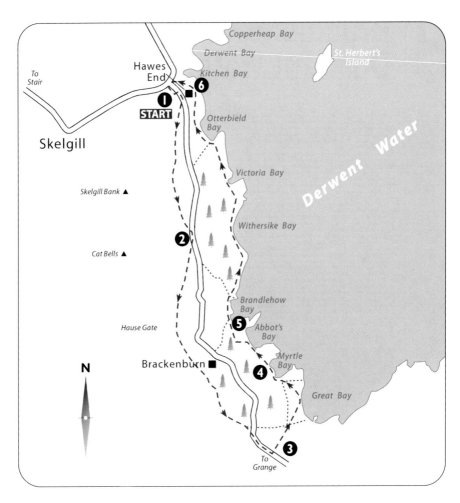

Introduction

When Brandlehow Woods came on the market in 1902, it was eyed as prime lakeside development land. Fortunately for us, the recently-founded National Trust got there first. Thanks to an appeal led by the local vicar, Canon Hardwicke Rawnsley, money was raised to purchase the woods and shoreline, the Trust's first acquisition in the Lake District. This walk takes you along that shoreline, in and out of Derwent Water's delightful bays. To begin with, though, you walk along a balcony path on the slopes of Cat Bells. Take your time along here to look back across the lake towards Keswick and the looming bulk of Skiddaw. It's a classic view, popular with photographers.

The Swinside Inn

The Swinside has long been a favourite with walkers and cyclists. To reach it, turn south-west off the road you have used from Portinscale. There's a large beer garden with great views over the Newlands Valley and surrounding fells. Inside you'll find a decent choice of real ales and a reliable menu, which takes in locally-caught fresh fish, as well as the usual Cumberland sausage and steak and Cumberland ale pie. Telephone: 017687 78253.

THE WALK

From the steep road bend at **Hawes End**, walk past the cattle grid, cutting the corner of the road to rejoin it when it has levelled out. Continue along the road for another 100 yards then take the obvious track rising up the hillside on the right.

This is an old miners' path connecting the various workings on this side of Cat Bells. The Brandlehow and Old Brandley mines produced lead until the 1890s.

Follow this excellent track as it contours along the side of the fell, gradually rising to some old mine workings, then gently dipping again. In about a mile, it drops all the way back down to the road by an old quarry, now used as a parking area.

Turn right along the road for a few paces, before veering right, up the track again as it continues along the side of the hill. After crossing three little becks, it rises round a bend and the road below you disappears behind a wooded garden.

There's a plaque on a crag here to Sir Hugh Walpole (1884–1941). His Herries Chronicles series of novels was set in this valley, and the author himself lived at Brackenburn Lodge, a house in the woods below you.

Beyond the plaque the path drops down to follow the wall in a narrow cleft. Ignore the gate into the woodland for cyclists and continue onto open fellside. You're joined from the right by the main track down from **Hause Gate** and the **Cat Bells** ridge. Descend through a gate and stile to the road. Turn right, with care, along the road.

After 150 yards turn left through a gate, signposted 'Lodore'. Walk along the excellent track over a pair of little wooden bridges to reach a kissing gate by the corner of a

Looking towards Skiddaw from the fellside above Brandlehow

wood. The track narrows, with the wood now on your left. In 50 yards go through another gate into a grassy area at the head of the lake. Bear left, picking out the planked sections to carry you over the bogs. Before you reach the lakeshore, you should intersect a more convincing gravel path and turn left along it. Another section of boardwalk carries you over the damp ground, then a clear and obvious track takes you over a rise and down to another section of boardwalk.

The leafy plant growing in profusion to your left is bog myrtle, appropriately enough, for this first little bay is called Myrtle Bay.

④

On the far side, go through a gate into woodland and continue on this path as it cuts off the headland separating **Myrtle Bay** from **Abbot's Bay**. The track swings left inland towards a stone cottage, **The Warren**. Turn right along the access track in front of the cottage and through a gateway. Take the left fork towards another cottage. Go through the kissing gate and follow the path between the house and its garage.

 ⑤

This next bay is **Brandlehow Bay**. Over a tiny footbridge, walk around the little stony beach and bear right, through a gate onto a stony headland. Continue along the beach to the jetty, then rise, away from the shore, into the trees.

The jetty is used by the Keswick Launch, which runs a frequent service around the lake. There are two more landing stages on this walk – at Low Brandlehow and Hawes End – so you could cruise for a while if your feet are sore. (Telephone: 017687 72263 for timetable.)

The path now follows the lakeshore, past **Withesike Bay** and **Victoria Bay**, before veering left through a gateway, cutting off the headland to reach **Otterbield Bay**. Through another gate the track veers right to a junction in front of buildings. Keep straight ahead, then choose the left-hand route in front of **Hawse End activity centre**.

 ⑥

Beyond the centre, a path turns off to the left, uphill and through trees. Follow this to emerge back on the road bend where you left your car.

9 | Around Buttermere

The view towards Honister across Buttermere

Distance 4¹/₂ miles 🕐 3 hours
Map: OS Explorer OL4 (GR 175170)

How to get there

Buttermere is 10 miles from Keswick over the Newlands Pass, or 15 miles if you go via the Honister Pass. For Newlands leave the A66 at Portinscale and follow the road through to the junction beyond Lingholm. Turn right, passing the Swinside Inn, then left when you get to the T-junction at Stair. This narrow road is very steep in places but it drops you down in Buttermere village at the roadside parking area above the church. **Parking:** On the roadside above the church or in the pay-and-display car parks past the Bridge Hotel.

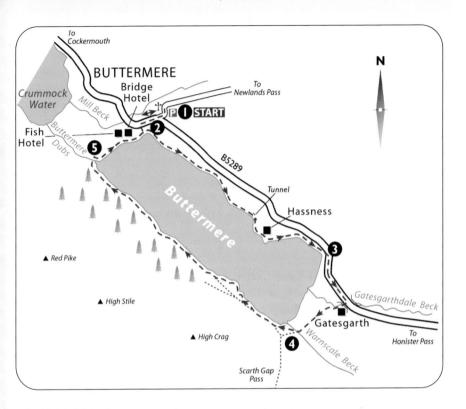

Introduction

Protected by a ring of mountain passes, Buttermere and its nearby sister, Crummock Water, reward the effort of visiting with magical views, whatever the weather. Caused by passing glaciers deepening the valley floor, there are dizzyingly steep mountain slopes on all sides, the head of the valley being terminated by the impressive crags of Fleetwith Pike and Haystacks – famed as the final destination of Alfred Wainwright's ashes. The well-known fell wanderer was not the only writer to be captivated by the beauty of the valley. In 1794, young Mary Robinson, the inn-keeper's daughter at the Fish, was immortalised in an early guidebook as the beautiful 'Maid of Buttermere'. This is a fairly easy walk, completing a circuit of the lake from the hamlet that shares its name.

The Bridge Hotel

Of Buttermere's two fine old inns, the Bridge takes pole position, by the main road. Bar meals for passing walkers include local sausage and salmon, Borrowdale trout and a warming Cumberland hot pot. They're fond of their Theakston's ale here as even in the more sedate dining room you'll find the venison with wild mushrooms has been slowly braised in Old Peculier. Telephone: 017687 70252.

THE WALK

 ①

Walk down past the church to the entrance to **Sykehouse Farm**, with its ice cream shop. Turn left and go through the farmyard, walking between the barn and a white farm building to a stile and gate. A level path leads across a field to a collection of gates. Take the right-hand gate, marked 'Shoreline path', down an enclosed path to another gate. Descend a short rocky stepped section and continue over a little bridge on the obvious path heading for the lake. Go through a gate and descend to the shoreline.

This path is by permission of the landowner, it's not a right of way. You enter the park of Hassness House, once the enviable mountain retreat of George Benson, a wealthy Manchester mill owner. For many years it has been a guest house operated by the commercial arm of the Ramblers' Association.

  ②

Follow the path to the left, through several gates, along the shore for over a mile. At one stage it disappears into a rocky tunnel, to emerge again on the other side above a small bay. Beyond this, the going is straightforward until a shaley track rises towards the road. Branch off to the right and stay with the narrower shoreline path through a gate and above a rocky outcrop. The going becomes a little muddy and eroded and eventually you must join the main road. The foreshore at the head of the lake has no public access.

The tunnel was built by Benson's estate workers so that he could complete a shoreline circuit of the lake on foot.

  ③

Turn right, along the road, for about 500 yards to **Gatesgarth Farm**. Cross over the bridge and turn right on a signposted track skirting the farmyard. In front of another bridge

Sourmilk Gill tumbles from the snowy heights of Red Pike, Buttermere

the bridleway points you left, through a gate. Beyond, bear right with a wall, passing a collection box for the local mountain rescue team. A straight path now leads over a bridge to a gate at the foot of the **Scarth Gap** track.

This is one of Lakeland's fine old trade routes, connecting the mountain core with the sea. Packhorses would once trail over this pass to the head of Ennerdale, then tackle the Black Sail Pass to descend to Wasdale and the ports at Whitehaven or Ravenglass.

Go through the gate and turn right, once more above the lakeshore. Stay with the lower path when you have the option, entering the woods beyond **Comb Beck**. The lakeside path continues to a pair of wooden bridges.

It is thought that the two lakes, Buttermere and Crummock, were once one. This silty land bridge between them is the product of centuries of farming exploiting the rich soil.

The second bridge is over **Buttermere Dubs**, the lake's outflow. Cross both bridges and turn right, to join the beachside path along the foot of the lake. At the end of the first field, go through a gate and continue. Towards the end of the beach, you cross a small stream and rise slightly to a gate. Through this you are able to intersect your outward route. Turn left and retrace your steps back into **Buttermere** village.

0 Borrowdale

Castle Crag, Borrowdale

Distance 4¹/₂ miles 🕐 3 hours
Map: OS Explorer OL4 (GR 245137)

How to get there

Take the B5289 Borrowdale road out of Keswick. Follow it for 7 miles to Seatoller village at the foot of the Honister Pass. **Parking:** There is a National Trust pay-and-display car park, with public toilets, on the right as you enter the village.

Drive and Stroll

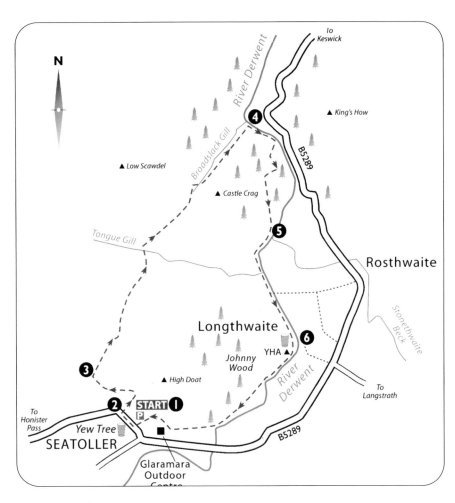

Introduction

After Eskdale, Borrowdale is my favourite Lakeland valley. This walk explores the middle of the dale, with the quarry-strewn slopes of Castle Crag as its centrepiece. This is not a place of high mountains, though they are often in view. Instead it is a walk of lower fellsides and rich woodland – if it looks 'picturesque' in places it's because this is the scenery that inspired this aesthetic ideal in the 18th century. Add a few cows by the water to your view and you have an oft-repeated image of the 'sublime'. Early tourists were keen to sketch the vista as seen through a tinted 'Claude glass', which gave them a wilder feel. I guess Photoshop plays a similar role now.

Honister's Yew Tree

Open between February and October, Tuesday to Sunday, the Yew Tree café and bar is strategically placed in the centre of Seatoller at the foot of the Honister Pass. Appropriately for a row of old quarrymen's cottages, they serve 'quarryman's food' by day – hot and cold sandwiches, chip butties, all-day breakfasts, pies and Cumberland sausage – but at night the owner's South African roots show, as the menu swings to specialities such as flame-frilled boerwors and bobotie (a South African chicken curry). Telephone: 017687 77634.

In winter months you might try the Scafell Hotel in Rosthwaite (tel. 01768 777208) or the Langstrath Country Inn at Stonewaite (tel. 01768 777239), both of which serve hearty bar meals.

THE WALK

From the car park, walk out to the road and turn right, up the hill through the village, passing the information centre and the **Yew Tree café**. By the warning signs for the pass ahead, turn right, through a gateway with stone pillars.

This is the old Honister toll road and it's now a permitted cycle route, so look out for mountain bikers descending at speed.

Ascend the track through a second gate and, as it bends left, go through another. Continue upwards on this rough track through another gate. As you round a bend, fork right up a grassy bank to a higher gate in a wall.

The old road stretches on up the pass to the slate workings that spill down to its summit. When the mines closed in 1986, after 300 years of continuous operation, it seemed likely that green slate would never again be extracted from Lakeland's fells. But, in 1997, they sprang back into life under new leaseholders as a heritage mine and today the business is still going strong.

Through the gate turn right, keeping the wall on your right. Pass through the gap between **Scawdel** and **High Doat**, continuing over two footbridges and through a gate before descending slightly and winding down to the beck. Cross the pair of bridges to emerge on a rocky path, which intersects a quarry track coming in from the left. Turn right and join a substantial track, now heading for the gap between **Castle Crag** and the fell. Descend to a gate into the woods, cross a bridge and continue descending to the river.

Castle Crag's summit is worth the scramble on a clear day for its dramatic views. At the top there is a memorial to John Hamer, in whose memory the crag was given to the National Trust, along with the other men of Borrowdale who died in the First World War. The slatey track can be loose though and there are some steep drops, so take care.

A fingerpost points you right, towards **Rosthwaite**, through a gate, to join a riverside path, now heading upstream. Shortly it dips back into the woods and a series of markers guides you through a tangle of crags, trees and old quarry workings.

One of the large disused workings above you was converted into a rudimentary home by the pioneering outdoor adventurer, Millican Dalton (1867–1947). Dalton left his job as a legal clerk in London in the 1890s to become a self-styled 'professor of adventure', offering guiding, climbing tuition, whitewater rafting

and other 'hair-breadth escapes'. He moved into the cave in the 1920s, spending his winters in a forest hut in the Chilterns. It was there he finally succumbed to pneumonia in the grim winter of 1947 after the hut burned down.

Return to the riverside and a gate leads out into open fields. A kissing gate lets you out of the wood into marshy pasture but the path remains obvious. Pass through a gate and stile on a farm track to a bridge. Stay on the right-hand side of the river, past the stepping stones and continuing on a levee.

At **Longthwaite's buildings** continue to the road by a bridge. Turn right and walk in front of the youth hostel, staying with the riverside path. A short section of slippery rocks is protected by a fixed metal chain. Round a rocky corner, go through a gate and skirt the base of the wood. As **Folly Bridge** comes into view, stay on the higher path, returning to the woods through a gap in the wall. Walk above the water treatment plant and round the back of the outdoor centre, ascending to a gate. Turn left to a stile and gate then join a track descending to the car park.

11 Rydal and Grasmere

The bridge over Rydal Beck at Rydal Hall

Distance 3¹/₂ miles 🕐 2 hours
Map: OS Explorer OL7 (GR 348066)

How to get there

The walk starts from White Moss Common, at the western end of Rydal Water. This is about halfway between Grasmere and Rydal villages on the A591. **Parking:** The pay-and-display car park operated by Lowther Estates at White Moss Common. There's a higher and a lower car park, and for this walk I'm assuming you'll park in the lower one.

Drive and Stroll

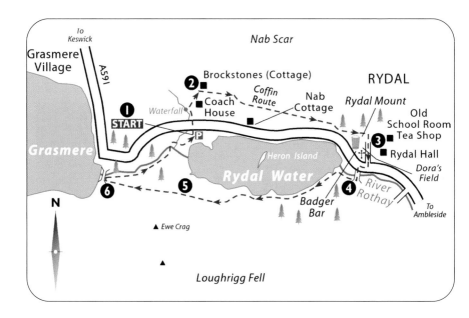

Introduction

Whether you're a fan of his poetry or not, it is hard to escape the impact of William Wordsworth on the central Lakes, and this walk explores the epicentre of that legacy. Essentially a circuit of Rydal Water, it begins on the old Coffin Route that connected Ambleside to the church at Grasmere, passes a former Wordsworth family home at Rydal Mount (and its more illustrious neighbour Rydal Hall), then returns by the lakeshore, before a final flourish gives a satisfying glimpse of Grasmere lake. It's mostly gentle, though there's a stiff, but brief, climb up a rough track to begin with.

The Old School Room Tea Shop, Rydal

Part way round the walk you come to the hamlet of Rydal. If it wasn't for the Wordsworth connection, it might be easily overlooked. It is mostly buildings associated with Rydal Hall, once the home of the Flemings and since 1970 a diocesan centre for the Bishop of Carlisle. At the back of the hall, on the continuation of the Coffin Route is a splendid tearoom, done up of late, but losing nothing of its simplicity in the process. There are home-made sandwiches and soup if you're hungry, but the real attraction is the cream tea with home-made scones, local damson jam and clotted cream. Telephone: 01539 432050 (Rydal Hall).

THE WALK

Cross the road from the lower car park to the post box opposite the toilets. From here a track runs in front of a house, going up the hill. Passing a waterfall on the left, continue to climb, now enclosed by walls. It's a little rough and steep in places, but this is definitely the hardest part of the walk and it doesn't last. At a pair of gates, pass through the one on the left and keep going up.

At the top, in front of an enviably-sited cottage, turn right along a path, contouring above a wall through a gate.

This is the old Coffin Route, the track used by burial parties from Ambleside to get to St Oswald's church in Grasmere in medieval times, before Ambleside had a church of its own. At several places along the route you'll see the large flat stones where the bearers rested their load en route.

Navigation is fairly simple, keeping to the left on the higher ground when the wall on your right drops to a corner. You pass through several more gates and, after a mile or so, you are funnelled onto an enclosed lane behind a house to join a road.

This is Rydal Mount, where William Wordsworth lived with his wife and family and his sister Dorothy, from 1813 to his death in 1850. They were tenants of the Flemings of Rydal Hall, the much larger country house you see across the road. This is where the poet completed most of his verse. He became 'Distributor of Stamps' for Westmorland in 1813, which secured him a small income, and from 1843 he was Poet Laureate. The house was bought by his great- great-granddaughter in 1969 and is now a museum.

Turn right down the hill. The **Old School Room Tea Shop** is at the back of **Rydal Hall** on the left. Continue down to the main road and turn right. Opposite the **Badger Bar**, cross the road and continue through a gate in the wall down to a bridge. Cross the bridge and turn right, along the riverbank.

Just beyond the church, you passed the entrance to Dora's Field. This was a plot of building land bought by the Wordsworths when it looked as if the Flemings would not renew their lease on Rydal Mount. Their eviction never materialised so William

Drive and Stroll

planted the land with daffodils in memory of his daughter Dora, who succumbed to tuberculosis in 1847.

🔖 ④

Keep to the right-hand path. Soon the river gives way to the shore of **Rydal Water** and through a gateway you enter **Rydal Woods**. Keep to the right-hand path for the views. Stay with the lower lakeside path, which becomes unexpectedly exciting where a little crag juts into the water. The view is broken for a while by a wall on your right, but the path rises above it and continues along the foot of the fell.

The Lion and the Lamb (rocky shapes on the summit of Helm Crag) come into view, then the path meanders away from the lake, beneath the towering slopes of Ewe Crag. You'll catch glimpses of quarry working all around you. The most dramatic remnant is Rydal Cave,

accessible from a higher path, where concerts have been held in the damp but spectacular interior. Most quarrying ceased in the 1920s.

🔖 ⑤

As you reach the woodland ignore a path through the wall on your right, but continue up to the brow of the hill ahead. Now take the lower path, heading for a bridge by **Grasmere lake's** outflow. It's worth crossing the bridge to get the view from the little craggy headland beyond, but the walk stays on this south side of the river.

🔖 ⑥

From the bridge follow the riverside path, which dips into the woodlands after 400 yards. Follow the river all the way to a bridge on the right. Cross this then turn right to follow the prominent path back to the toilets and car park at **White Moss**.

2 | Crosby Ravensworth

Down the road from Dalebanks in Crosby Ravensworth

Distance 4¹/₂ miles 🕐 2¹/₂ hours
Map: OS Explorer OL19 (GR 621147)

How to get there

Crosby Ravensworth is between Appleby and Shap in the Lyvennet Valley. Probably the swiftest approach is from the M6 at Shap. From junction 39, drive into Shap and at the south end of the village, a right turn is signposted to Crosby Ravensworth. This brings you, in about 4 miles, to the village centre, with the church to your left and the pub to your right. **Parking:** There is roadside parking towards the church.

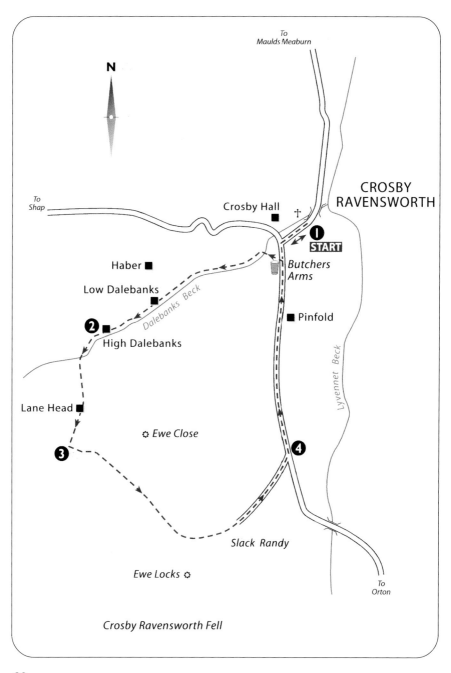

To
Maulds Meaburn

N

CROSBY
RAVENSWORTH

To
Shap

Crosby Hall

START

Haber

Butchers
Arms

Low Dalebanks

Dalebanks Beck

Pinfold

High Dalebanks

Lyvennet Beck

Lane Head

Ewe Close

Slack Randy

Ewe Locks

To
Orton

Crosby Ravensworth Fell

Introduction

I think the Lyvennet Valley is one of Cumbria's best-kept secrets. The little Lyvennet Beck rises on the wild moors of Crosby Ravensworth Fell and winds through a quiet dale of scattered farms and delightful villages before joining the Eden near Temple Sowerby. It wasn't always so overlooked. A Roman road passes this way from the fort at Tebay and there are many traces of pre- and post-Roman settlements. In 1651 Charles II marched his Scottish army through here on their way to defeat by Cromwell at Worcester. This walk follows Dalebanks Beck, a tributary of the Lyvennet, from Crosby Ravensworth up onto the fell, before descending again by the giant sheep-gathering funnel known as Slack Randy. There are some very muddy sections, making wellies the recommended footwear.

The Butchers Arms

Possibly taking its name from the Duke of Cumberland, the 'Butcher' of Culloden, this quiet village inn concentrates on cooking simple food well. Alongside a couple of real ales (sometimes including beers from the local Tirril Brewery) expect specials like salmon and dill fishcakes, roast beef and rack of lamb to supplement the bar food standards. Telephone: 01931 715202.

THE WALK

①

Facing the bus shelter at the centre of the village, turn left and walk up the road towards the pub.

Crosby Hall, across the beck from the start of the walk, was the scene of a notorious murder in 1286, when Robert de Appleby killed Nicholas de Hastings at the gate of his brother's house.

Turn right, beside the **Butchers Arms**, down a track to cross a footbridge. On the far side turn left

along a lane, passing some children's swings. Cross a cattle bridge and continue on this surfaced lane to **Low Dalebanks**, then continuing to **High Dalebanks**.

At Low Dalebanks the Roman Wicker Street crossed the beck on its way up to Wickerslack and beyond to Brougham.

②

Keep to the right of the farm buildings to find a footpath sign above some old buildings. Go through a gate and walk along the track. At the far end of the wall on your left, a faint track dives down

A bridge over Dalebanks Beck in Crosby Ravensworth

into the valley to cross the beck by a bridge. On the far side a stile leads into a field. Bear half right up the bank, picking off a diagonal line across the field to the ruins of an old farmyard. In the yard, turn right through a gate in front of the old house, then turn left up the extremely muddy lonning (farm track) through another deserted farmyard (you may find it expedient to walk up the adjacent field). At the gate at the top walk out onto the open fell.

Away in the fields to your left you may be able to discern the low banks and hollows of the Romano-British settlement at Ewe Close. This is just one of a number of pre-English sites in the valley that have led some to speculate that Crosby Ravensworth was once the royal seat of Urien of Rheged, the Celtic kingdom that flourished here in what is often referred to as the 'Dark Ages'. The evidence is sketchy, but the 6th-century court poet Taliesin wrote of his royal sponsor as the 'Lord of bright Llwyfenydd'. Another site at Ewe Locks is scattered amongst the remains of medieval shielings at the top of Slack Randy.

Turn left, following a path that aims across the fell to intersect a wall

coming up from the left in about 400 yards. Follow this track now, staying roughly parallel with the walls on your left. The route loops round to the left, joining other tracks coming from across the fell. Heading down the slope you are funnelled into the tapering walls of **Slack Randy**. Eventually the track becomes a metalled lane to a cattle grid and delivers you at the edge of the village.

A slack is a hollow on a hill slope in Old Norse (slakki). Here it has been adapted as an 'outgang' with walls funnelling in from the open fell to collect sheep.

Turn left and walk along the road, passing the **Goldsworthy Pinfold** on the right and the **Butchers Arms** to reach your car.

The cone in the pinfold is one of 46 sculptures built around the county between 1996 and 2003 by the renowned artist Andy Goldsworthy. St Lawrence's church seems huge for such a small village. It has ancient origins – the remnants of a 7th-century cross can be seen in the churchyard – but it was heavily restored by Sir Robert Smirke under guidance from the Lowther family in the early 1800s.

13 Smardale Gill and Fell

Distance 5½ miles 🕐 3 hours
Map: OS Explorer OL19 (GR 739082)

How to get there

Turn off the A685 just 2 miles south-west of Kirkby Stephen. Ignore the turning to Waitby. Cross over the railway and turn left at the junction. Ignore the sign for Smardale, continuing straight ahead over the old railway line. Turn left immediately and then left again by the grassy triangle to a parking area in front of a dismantled rail bridge. **Parking:** There is a small parking area at the Smardale end of the nature reserve.

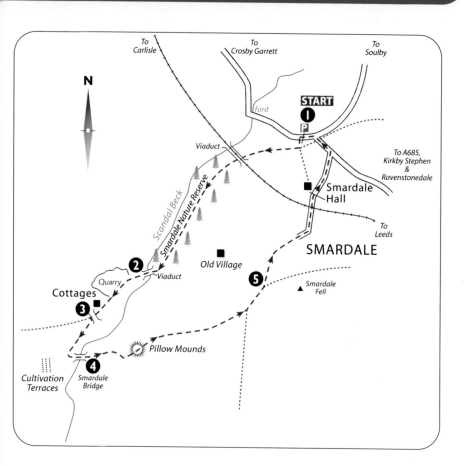

Introduction

The South Durham and Lancashire Union Railway ran from Darlington to Tebay, linking the coke works of the north-east with the steelworks and iron ore mines of west Cumberland. Built in 1861, it was soon absorbed by the North Eastern Railway. It carried trains until 1961 when British Railways closed it, quickly pulling up the rails and demolishing several bridges. Fortunately for us they left the dramatic section through remote Smardale virtually intact and by the 1990s it had become a magnificent walkway through a nationally important nature reserve. If you don't fancy the return route over the fell, you can turn round and walk back the way you came on this dramatic slice of Victorian railway building.

Drive and Stroll

The Black Swan, Ravenstonedale

There are no pubs or teashops near this walk, but you're only a few minutes' drive from Kirkby Stephen or from Ravenstonedale (reached southwards along the A685). In the latter you'll find the Black Swan Hotel, a comfortable village inn that has been gobbling up awards for its beer and hospitality of late. Wash down the local trout fishcakes with a pint of Hawkshead Gold, or snack on goat's cheese paninis, with a robust cappuccino. Telephone: 01539 623204.

THE WALK

---

①

From the car park, go through the gate opposite and walk up the embankment past the nature reserve information boards to join the disused railway trackbed. Turn right and from here navigation is very simple, following the disused line for about 2½ miles.

After the first straight (you might notice a plaque marking the site of a crash in 1955, halfway along) you pass under the Smardale viaduct – a magnificent 12-arch giant carrying the Settle–Carlisle railway 130 ft above Scandal Beck.

 ②

In another mile or so you come to a second impressive bridging of the gorge, **Smardale Gill viaduct**, this time carrying the line you are on. Walk across the viaduct and continue along the trackbed, passing the

Smardale lime kilns and a pair of abandoned lineside cottages.

The limestone which fed the kilns is also the defining characteristic of the nature reserve. The grassland is dominated by blue moor-grass, with pockets of alpine bistort and bloody cranesbill, bird's-eye primrose and butterfly orchid. The woods are now coppiced on a 20-year rotation.

 ③

Pass beneath a small bridge and immediately turn left up the embankment to a stile. Over this, turn right, now on the line of the **Coast to Coast** walk. Descend towards the bottom of the valley, forking left about halfway down the field to reach **Smardale Bridge**. Turn right, through a gate.

This packhorse bridge was once a lot less remote than it now seems. In 1663 it was the unlikely meeting place for the 'Kaber Rigg plot', a group of disaffected dissenters rebelling against the restoration of Charles II. Their protest quickly

Smardalegill Viaduct

fizzled out and the ringleaders were executed at Appleby. There is evidence that there was once an inn here, but the remains are a bit sketchy. More prominent are the many remnants of much earlier cultures. The hill rising to the west of the bridge is clearly marked by cultivation terraces, which may be well over 1,000 years old. Higher up the hill you traverse a series of 'pillow mounds', medieval warrens used for farming rabbits.

 ④

Ascend the broad track to cross **Smardale Fell**. Beyond a fence and gate it takes a wide sweep to the left. As **Smardale** disappears from view to the left, you reach the fell gate. Beyond this a rutted track crosses the open fell, running parallel with the wall on your left. Ignore a gate in the wall to your left and continue down to a four-way fingerpost in a dip.

 ⑤

Take the left-hand track, staying close to the wall over the brow of the rise then descending through three fields to a small group of cottages at the end of a surfaced track. Go through the gate and follow the road under the bridge and past **Smardale Hall** to a junction. Turn left along the road, crossing the line of the disused railway. Turn left and left again to reach your car.

Smardale Hall is a medieval 'hall house' built over a previous pele tower, though its turrets may be more recent fanciful additions. There are traces of further fortifications in the grounds. As you approach the modern village, the site of a previous settlement abandoned in the 12th century can be discerned in the fields to your left.

67

14 Eskdale and Stanley Ghyll Force

Distance 3 miles 🕐 2 hours
Map: OS Explorer OL6 (GR 171002)

How to get there

Unless you're based in West Cumbria already, there are few easy ways to Eskdale. The valley is usually approached from the A595, either from Broughton-in-Furness, passing through Ulpha and traversing Birker Fell, or from Gosforth in the north. Both routes converge on the King George IV pub in Eskdale Green. Follow the signs to Boot, but a few hundred yards beyond Stanley Ghyll House, turn right on a narrow lane over a bridge. The car park is on the left a bit further on. From the central Lakes you may like to try the Wrynose and Hardknott Passes, but they are severe roads and not for nervous drivers. **Parking:** Free car park at Trough House Bridge, Dalegarth.

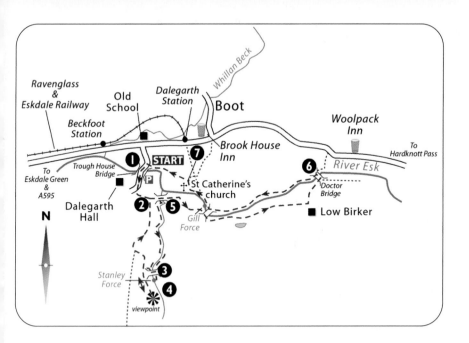

Introduction

This is a superb, gentle walk in my favourite Lakeland dale. It begins with the spectacular gorge of Stanley Ghyll and its waterfall before following an ancient bridleway up the dale to Doctor Bridge, then returning on a riverside path to pretty little St Catherine's church, across the fields from Boot. It's good for any weather (in fact the falls are best seen in or just after rain), and the glimpses of the high mountains rising around the head of the valley are magnificent. Stanley Ghyll itself can be slippery underfoot and some of the track has fallen away recently, but the access is still relatively straightforward – take heed of the warning notices though.

The Brook House Inn

You can see the three-storey, whitewashed Brook House Inn across the fields towards the end of the walk. It's well worth a diversion, and is an excellent end-of-walk dining venue. In addition to the range of real ales, sandwiches and filled ciabattas and an enormous selection of malt whiskies, you can get stuck into duck breast with plum and orange sauce, grilled sea bass, or a Moroccan vegetable and bean casserole. Telephone: 01946 723288.

THE WALK

①

Walk out onto the lane and turn left, then left again at the junction for **Dalegarth Hall**. Go through a gate and continue on up the track. In about 50 yards, at a crossways, go straight ahead, signposted 'the waterfalls, Stanley Ghyll and Birker Fell'.

Dalegarth Hall, with its distinctive round chimneys, dates from the 16th century and was home to the landowning Stanley family.

  ②

Turn left through a gate into **Stanley Ghyll** and continue to the bank of the beck. Turn right and head upstream on an obvious path as the ravine closes in around you. Rounding a corner, steps lead up to a wooden bridge, beyond which the path continues on the opposite bank. A little further on, a second bridge takes you back again, now in a steep-sided gorge. Stone steps lead to a junction and a third bridge. Cross the bridge and ascend the path, with care, for a view of the plunge pool and waterfall.

  ③

Returning to the third bridge, now take the higher, left-hand path at the junction beneath a fallen tree and rising out of the gorge. The path levels by a stone bridge and another junction. Turn left and continue climbing up through the woods to the ravine viewing area.

Take care! The drop here is 150 ft and there is no safety barrier.

  ④

Return down through the wood to the stone bridge passed earlier. Cross it again but take the path straight ahead, then bear left through the woods to a gate in the wall. Pass through this into open country, intersecting the old lane to **Birker Fell**. Turn right, down the lane, to return to the gate into **Stanley Ghyll** you passed earlier. Go through the gate again, but this time, turn left, down the hill, to meet the bridleway as it reaches a ford and narrow bridge.

  ⑤

Cross the bridge and leave the woodland through the gate on the far side. Fork right now, through the bracken, with the distinctive profile of **Hartley and Gate crags** ahead of you. At a junction of paths and by a gap in the wall bear right, around the wall corner and, at the next junction, go with the blue arrow through another gate and stile. The easy path leads you past a little tarn on the right behind pine trees. Beyond this you continue to the old farmstead at **Low Birker**, now being restored. Turn left here in front of the farm buildings and descend on the access track towards the river. Eventually you will come to **Doctor Bridge**.

Under the arch you can see where this old packhorse bridge was widened to allow the eponymous doctor's carriage to cross.

Cross the bridge and turn left, now on the opposite bank of the **Esk**. Follow the riverside path, sometimes enclosed between walls, until, just after a gate, you see a bridge down to your left. Drop down to the riverbank here, but don't cross the bridge. Instead bear right, following the old railway trackbed. Where this heads into an enclosed lane, turn left through a gate to reach **St Catherine's church**, next to the stepping stones.

The railway trackbed brought La'al Ratty (the local name for Eskdale's

narrow-gauge railway) to the Gill Force and Gate Crag iron ore mines from the 1880s. The church is much older, probably being established by the prior of St Bees in the 12th century. It was promoted to parish status following local protest to the Pope in 1445 about the journey to St Bees for burials and baptisms. 'Restoration' in 1881 was not as damaging as some Victorian efforts, but the bells and the font are probably the most notably ancient things remaining.

Turn right, up the lane, then after 100 yards turn left, along an enclosed track. This leads all the way back to the road above **Trough House Bridge**. Turn left and cross the bridge back to your car.

Beneath the bridge (pronounced 'Troffus' Bridge) the Esk is channelled into a narrow deep pool. This is popular with outdoor education groups and achieved minor fame in the 1980s in the Julie Walters drama She'll Be Wearing Pink Pyjamas.

15 Coniston

Distance 5 miles 🕒 3 hours
Map: OS Explorer OL6 and OL7 (GR 303975)

How to get there

Coniston is 8 miles south-west of Ambleside, on the A593. From junction 36 on the M6 you can follow the A590 and then the A591 to Ambleside, or take the A590 through Newby Bridge to Greenodd, then the A5084 north to meet the A593 at Torver just south of the village. **Parking:** There is a pay-and-display car park, with public toilets, by the tourist information centre. If you're coming from Ambleside it's signposted on the left just past the row of shops.

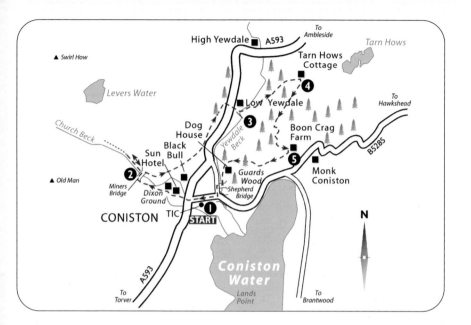

Introduction

Coniston is a busy little village that has managed to maintain its character despite the annual onslaught of tourists. Visitors are usually interested in three things here – the lake, the Old Man, and Tarn Hows. This walk addresses all three without actually visiting them; as a consequence it shows a much quieter side to the village. We see the Old Man from below, and perhaps conclude that Swirl How, though lower in height, is just as dramatic. We don't see Tarn Hows, but we do get to the idyllic cottage that donated its name to the nearby honeypot. We don't dip our toes in the water but we do see the lake from above Boon Crag, possibly one of the best vantage points from which to appreciate its silvery form.

The Black Bull Inn

You're spoiled for choice when it comes to refreshments in Coniston village. The Black Bull distinguishes itself by brewing its own beer (its Bluebird Bitter has been a CAMRA champion). Inside this 400-year-old coaching inn, you can eat local Woodalls beer sausages or shoulder of local lamb, or pick from the vegetarian specials by open fires on cold days and under aged beams that have seen artistic and literary giants such as Turner, Coleridge and de Quincy pass through the bar. Telephone: 01539 441335.

THE WALK

From the tourist information centre, turn left up to the main street. Cross the bridge and turn immediately right up the lane, following signs for the **Sun Hotel**. When you reach the pub, turn right, signposted 'The Old Man and Levers Water', through a gate by **Dixon Ground Farm**.

The large peak ahead of you is Swirl How. Church Beck has recently returned to electricity generating after a gap of 40 years. The Coniston Hydro Scheme opened in 2007, producing enough electricity to power 300 homes.

On the far side of the field cross a bridge and ascend the bank, continuing on the rough track through a kissing gate to **Miners Bridge**.

Cross the bridge and turn left for a few hundred yards to view **Copper Mines Valley**.

This was where Coniston's mineral wealth lay. Early copper and silver extraction in Elizabethan times was followed by more extensive mining in the 18th century. But the real change came with the arrival of renowned engineer John Taylor in 1825. He built complex drainage systems to make even the deepest ore deposits accessible, which prompted the railway's expansion to the village in 1859. The glory days were over by 1897, and by the end of the First World War most of the machinery had been taken for scrap. Now the mine buildings are holiday accommodation, including a youth hostel.

Return to **Miners Bridge** but stay on the descending track to a gate on the left. Go through this and follow this permissive bridleway for over a mile until a ramp allows you to cross the road.

Follow the access road to **Low Yewdale** and walk to the right of the barns. Cross the bridge and immediately turn left through a gate on a riverside path into woodland. It climbs away from the beck into the forest, where it joins a track from the right. Continue up the hill, until, just over the brow, a pair of gates lead to **Tarn Hows Cottage**.

This pretty former farm was part of the Monk Coniston Estate bought by Beatrix Potter and is now a private house, though owned by the National Trust.

Coniston tourist information centre

↴ ④

Turn right here, through a gate, then right again at the bend to join a grassy path across a field. The field path descends to a gate and stile where a fantastic view of the lake opens up.

The Monk Coniston Estate was owned by the Marshall family of Holbeck in Leeds, whose fortune came from flax spinning (Marshall's Mill employed over 2,000 people). James Garth Marshall (1802–1873) embarked on an ambitious landscaping programme, including the damming of three tarns to make Tarn Hows. Their Lakeland home was at Monk Coniston, seen in the trees down to your left. When Beatrix Potter acquired the estate in 1930, she immediately gave this part to the National Trust, who, in turn, leased the house to the Holiday Fellowship. As HF Holidays Ltd they are still the Trust's tenants here.

Continue the winding descent to reach a gate and join the track down towards **Boon Crag**.

↴ ⑤

Before you get to the farm, turn right, over a stile, and walk up the path into **Guards Wood**. Enter the wood and follow the path over the crest, then steeply down to a gate. Beyond this a path slips between the wall and gorse bushes to join another descending route. Go through a gate and past the restored **Dog House** on the left. The track continues to a bridge by the sports ground. Over the bridge, turn left down the road, turning right at the bottom to return to the car park.

16 Claife's Heights above Windermere

Looking across Mitchell Wyke to Ferry House

Distance 4 miles 🕐 2¹/₂ hours
Map: OS Explorer OL7 (GR 387960)

How to get there

Approach from Hawkshead on the B5285, or from the Windermere ferry, which connects to the A592 just south of Bowness-on-Windermere. From the ferry, drive past Ferry House and take the first right towards Harrow Slack. **Parking:** There is a National Trust pay-and-display car park, on the left after about 400 yards.

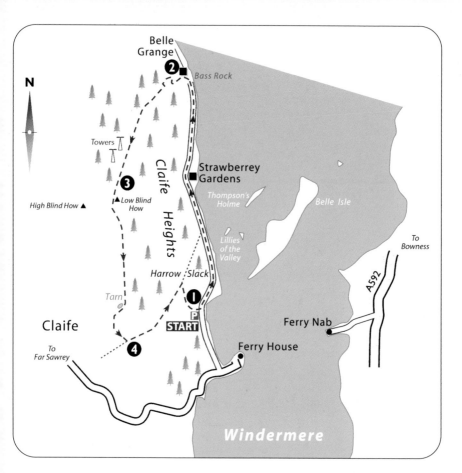

Introduction

A ferry ride makes a fine start to any walk and this is no exception. There have been ferries crossing Windermere here since medieval times and their stories have merged into the landscape of this western shore. Here in Claife's woodlands, you may be stalked by the sinister presence of the Crier. The legend goes that the ferrymen were taunted by a voice late at night, crying 'Boat! Boat!' from the Claife bank. A young crewman braved the night crossing, only to return, pale and speechless, dying the next day. A monk was called to exorcise the demon, and succeeded in banishing it to the woods and quarries 'until men should walk dryshod across the lake'. Follow this delightful woodland walk later in the day, as the light fades and you may quickly believe in the haunted tale.

77

Drive and Stroll

The Claife Crier Bar

Taking its name from the ghostly howler of the nearby fell, this is the public bar of the Sawrey Hotel at Far Sawrey and is the nearest refreshment venue to the start of the walk on the Hawkshead side of the ferry. Inside it is cosy with low ceilings, open fires and a wide range of real ales, including local Hawkshead brews. Try the local venison sausage for a change, grilled Esthwaite trout, or a wild rice, spinach and honey nut roast. Telephone: 01539 443425.

THE WALK

From the car park, turn left along the road, following it along the shore until it runs out at a cattle grid.

Of the view of the lake from here, with its tangle of islands and inlets, Thomas West's 1778 guide said 'a sweeter picture than this the lake does not furnish'.

Continue on this wide track, passing **Strawberry Gardens**, then rising into the woods and dipping once more to the shore. Eventually, near a boatshed on the right, you leave the lakeshore as a walled enclosure comes between you and the lake. Take the track to the left, signposted to Hawkshead, which proceeds through a barrier and begins to ascend on stone setts by the side of the garden of **Belle Grange**.

Much of the Claife Estate was owned by the Curwen family of Workington Hall, on the west coast. They purchased the Round House on Belle Isle in 1781 and set about transforming the landscape to conform with prevailing concepts of the picturesque. Their pride and joy was Claife Station, not a halt for trains, but a viewing house, where visitors could peer at lake and woods through different tints of stained glass. The station's evocative ruins can be found above the road, a few hundred yards from Ferry House. The estate is now cared for by the National Trust.

A series of zigzags takes you up into the woods. Where they level off, turn left on the path signposted to Far Sawrey and Low Blind How. Cross a little ford and ignore the path dropping down to the left, instead continuing uphill following the yellow arrow.

The track levels out just below the crest of the ridge and clearings in

Claife's woodlands along the shore

the trees give you magnificent views over the lake to Bowness, Windermere town and the fells beyond.

Follow the path as it dives right, into the conifer wood, but stay left at a junction of paths as you come round the summit of **Low Blind How**.

If you're going to meet the Crier, surely it is up here amongst the crags and dense forest. But if you hear a rustle it is more likely to be a roe deer, startled by your intrusion on this remote domain.

Descend to a wall below some overgrown crags and, as the path rises again, it is now enclosed by a wall and deer fence. Rise again; this time a gate leads onto rough grazing land. Keep the wall on your left as you pass tiny **Scale Ivy Tarn** (you may have to divert here if the water level is over the track). The track becomes enclosed again, finally descending to a junction.

④

Turn left on the bridleway, toward **Windermere lakeshore** and ferry. Ignore the first turning off to the right, and enter the woods through a gate. In about 400 yards, another track leads down to the right. Follow this back to the car park.

17 Orrest Head

Distance 3¹/₂ miles 🕐 2 hours
Map: OS Explorer OL7 (GR 416986)

How to get there

Windermere town is 15 miles from the M6 at junction 36, on the A591.
Parking: There are a couple of free roadside parking areas (one is disk parking) on the edge of town on the A591, above the station on the right (approaching from Kendal). If these are full, there is pay-and-display parking around the station.

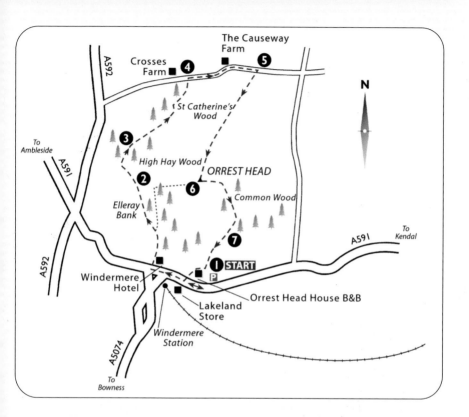

Introduction

This simple walk has introduced many people to the Lake District. A young Alfred Wainwright first stepped off the train at Windermere station in 1931 and was captivated by the view from Orrest Head's rocky summit. The Lakeland Fells that spread before him from this modest viewpoint were to change his life forever. It was the arrival of the railway in 1844 that created Windermere town. As you leave the junction by the railway's vast hotel you'll pass many of the opulent villas built by the first wave of incomers around that time. Higher up you pass through National Trust woodland before climbing above the trees for that life-changing vista of fells rising above the far side of the lake.

Drive and Stroll

Lakeland Café

This definitely isn't the usual walkers' boots and bobble hats tearoom. But, that said, the first floor café above the Lakeland kitchenware shop (on the south side of the A591 – see map) isn't the usual in-store restaurant either. Run by three-Michelin star winning chef Steven Doherty (perhaps best known for his supreme pub fare at the Punch Bowl at Crosthwaite), the food is simple – filled baguettes, salads, wraps, nice puds – but astonishingly well delivered. Call ahead to guarantee a seat. Telephone: 01539 447116.

THE WALK

From the lay-by, cross the road and walk down the hill towards the station. Cross back over in front of the **Windermere Hotel**, picking out a driveway to the left of the hotel with a large sign pointing to **Orrest Head**. Walk along the driveway for 50 yards before turning left along a snicket, now ignoring the sign to Orrest Head viewpoint. Follow this enclosed path between gardens to a junction. Take the left-hand path, dropping down to cross an access road and continuing on a narrow path bounded by an iron railing.

There are wonderful views across the lake from here, to the wooded heights of Claife and beyond to the Coniston Fells.

The path emerges on a surfaced lane. Turn right and, at the entrance to **Elleray Bank**, take the path on the left, which continues between the walls of grand villa gardens. Cross an access road and continue until the woodland on the right opens out. Where the path dips slightly to a footpath sign, go right on a permissive path through a gate into the woods. Continue on this path to another gate to emerge in a field.

Maintain your direction across the field, now walking parallel with a woodland wall on your right. Don't be drawn down to the bridge on your left but ascend to a gate in the far right-hand corner of the field. Through this, keep to the wall on your left until a kissing gate leads you into woods. Ignore a path coming up from the left and continue on the woodland path to cross a wooden bridge. Beyond this the path reaches another kissing gate leading out onto a minor road.

Turn right and follow the road with care for about 400 yards past **Causeway Farm** to a stone stile and footpath sign on the right.

Cross the stile and follow the path beyond over a tiny bridge. Maintain your direction, to the left of a transmission pole. In this rising craggy field, you're steering a middle course, on a faint path, running parallel with the wall, up the centre of the field. The path's identity becomes more pronounced as you weave between thorn and holly bushes, levelling out to reach a gate and the top of a new access track. Now a winding path leads up through the scrub to the summit of **Orrest Head**.

There are so many benches here, it's a wonder there's space left for the actual summit. A topograph explains the view, which is vast. It's a captivating spot. Nearly 100 years before the 23-year-old Wainwright stumbled off the train, Wordsworth was incensed at the encroaching modernity. 'Is then no nook of English ground secure from rash assault?' he wrote in October 1844, in his poem On The Projected Kendal and Windermere *Railway in 1844. Now we look kindly on our meagre little trains and it is cars and lorries on the A591 you can hear.*

With your back to **Windermere lake**, pick out a descending track from the summit, which quickly steepens into woodland, ducking beneath the branches of an ancient yew tree. A stone stile takes you to a walled lane and a right turn leads straight to a gate back into woodland. The track continues to descend, and a gap in the wall leads to a fingerpost. Ignore the left turn, maintaining your direction on the track signed to the A591 and Windermere. The path concludes at a gate into a field with a warning sign about suckler cattle.

Enter the field and descend by the wall on the right. As you approach a white building in the trees ahead, you are funnelled into a walled trackway. Pass through a gate and carry on down the lane to emerge on the main road by the **Windermere Hotel**. If you left your car in the lay-by, it is up to the left from here, otherwise go straight across to the station, Booths and Lakeland.

18 Whitbarrow's Township Allotment

Distance 4 miles 🕐 2¹/₂ hours
Map: OS Explorer OL7 (GR 449894)

How to get there

From junction 36 on the M6 take the A590 towards Kendal, staying on this road and heading for Barrow-in-Furness at the A591 intersection. Turn right by the Gilpin Bridge Inn onto the A5074. There is a turning off to The Row in another 3 miles. Pass through the village to the road end. **Parking:** There is limited roadside parking at the road end beyond The Row. Alternative parking can be found opposite the Lyth Valley Bar and Restaurant on the main road.

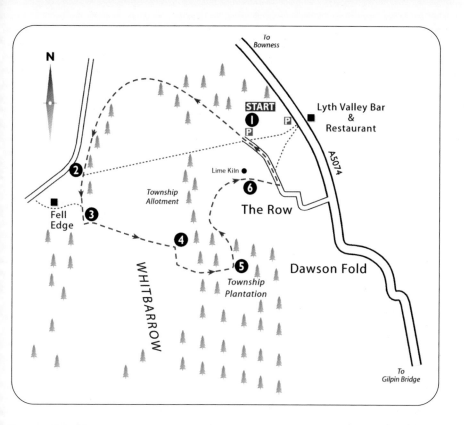

Introduction

The huge scarp of Whitbarrow is one of the first hills many visitors to Lakeland see. It rises up from the flatlands of the Lyth and Kent valleys, presenting a forbidding aspect. From the main road it's not immediately apparent how you gain its presumably sylvan upper reaches. This walk takes you over the northern end of the escarpment, across the tract of rough grazing land known as Township Allotment. The name goes back to the enclosure of Heversham parish in 1815, when this difficult limestone upland remained one of the few sheep pastures left amidst the newly regimented and drained fields of the valley floor. Now it is an important wildlife reserve (the land around the south and centre of the hill is a National Nature Reserve).

The Lyth Valley Bar and Restaurant

By the roadside on the A5074, the Lyth Valley is a smart bar and restaurant with airy rooms overlooking 'Damson Country'. The bar menu includes deep-fried Brie with a damson chutney, home-made salmon fishcakes, bangers and mash and good selection of lunchtime sandwiches; a children's menu is also available. There's usually a real ale on offer, and you can even get a latte or a cappuccino. You'll have to leave your muddy boots and waterproofs by the door though. Telephone: 01539 568233.

THE WALK

From the road end, take the byway signposted 'Witherslack Road'. After about ¾ mile go through a gate and continue on the broad track, now with open country up to your left. Keep to the edge of the fell by a wall as the path dips again; you are now on the far side of **Whitbarrow**. Pass a large water trough and continue along the fell foot track through two gates to a junction.

The Winster valley comes into view below you here. Across the fields you may be able to spy Cowmire Hall, originally a 16th-century pele tower, with 17th-century additions, giving it an imposing three-storey presence.

Leave the byway for the fell foot bridleway, through a gate ahead of you. Leave this as it dips right, into a field, and stay with the edge of

the fell, now on a narrow path against the fence.

The geology changes here as you set foot on the scarp slope. Below you is shale, but from now on you will be on limestone. The effect of this change can be seen in the vegetation. In spring especially, you'll see daffodils and primroses up the hill, but bluebells and wood anemones lower down.

A track joins you from **Fell Edge Farm** on your right and the path begins to rise into the woods. It narrows and steepens beneath overhanging trees and crosses a little beck at the spring line before a series of zigzags takes you steeply up the scarp to a wall and stile.

Cross this and on the open fell beyond walk straight ahead, on a winding path heading for the brow of the hill. As you approach a line of limestone scar ignore crossing paths and keep ahead. On reaching the brow, a view of the **Lyth valley**

Whitbarrow

opens out ahead of you. Ignore a crossing path and continue ahead, descending to a little dip.

The open plateau is dominated by limestone, though here the pavements are not so well defined as they are further south on Whitbarrow. This area was heavily quarried, a particular use for the stone being grinding wheels for the local gunpowder works. Though softer, limestone is less prone to sparks than the more conventional millstone grit.

 ④

A white arrow points you right, down a descending track towards the tree line. At another post join a larger track down to a gate and into the woods. Keep going down, ignoring options to left and right.

Much of the forestry on this side of the hill was planted in 1919. The Forestry Commission began working here in 1955.

 ⑤

Eventually you reach a complex path junction with a signpost. Turn left and maintain your direction on the middle track, again ignoring options to left and right, now contouring round to the left. Stay with a wall on your right, as the path bends right to a gate out of the woods. Stay with the right-hand wall through the large field, curving all the way round to descend into **The Row** at a gate below the lime kiln.

The lime kiln is particularly well preserved. The lime produced would have been used locally to improve the soil for agriculture.

 ⑥

In the hamlet walk down to the road and turn left to return to your car or keep ahead on a descending bridleway if you left your car at the **Lyth Valley Bar**.

19 Dent and the Dales Way

Distance 4 miles 🕐 2¹/₂ hours
Map: OS Explorer OL2 (GR 703871)

How to get there

Dent is 10 miles from junction 37 on the M6. Drive to Sedbergh on the A684. As you approach the town turn right, following the signs for Dent. Turn right again at the T-junction and follow the winding road for about 6 miles. **Parking:** There is a pay-and-display car park next to the public toilets on the left as you enter the village.

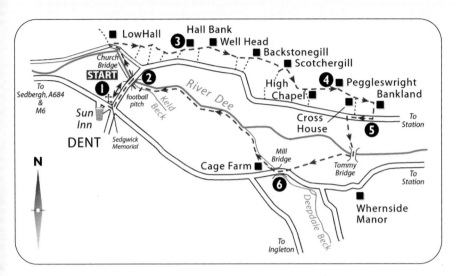

Introduction

This is a typical Dales walk, connecting a string of spring-line farmsteads on the north side of the valley, before returning to the cobbled streets of Dent town along the Dales Way. It's a fairly easy walk, though you'll have to concentrate on navigating to pick out all the stiles between the fields in the first part. It's also very much a Yorkshire walk, although Dent and the neighbouring parishes of Sedbergh and Garsdale have been in Cumbria since 1974. The village's most famous son was Adam Sedgwick (1785–1873), a pioneering geologist who went on from the village school to be a spellbinding lecturer and professor of earth science at Cambridge University. Charles Darwin was one of his pupils.

The Sun Inn

This legendary village pub has ancient coin-studded beams and open coal fires to keep out the winter chill. It was the original outlet for the Dent Brewery before it moved to larger premises at Cowgill to deal with widespread demand, and the pub is still owned by the tiny brewer. The food is basic but wholesome and locally sourced wherever possible, and there are veggie options. Telephone: 01539 625208.

Drive and Stroll

THE WALK

From the car park entrance, turn left and walk up the cobbled street, bearing left along an enclosed path into the churchyard.

In the old bier room to the side of the church you'll find the Discover Dentdale exhibition, which explains the history of this lovely valley and has a video about its people and their lives. St Andrew's church has Norman origins and was substantially rebuilt in 1417.

On the far side of the churchyard, descend the steps to the road and turn left to the bridge.

Beyond the bridge turn left through a stile and go down steps into a field. Follow the path to the far end, where it rises to another stile onto a lane. Turn left for a couple of hundred paces, then turn right towards **Low Hall**. Immediately turn right though a tiny stile into a field. Walk back parallel with the way you've just come, then go through two gates and aim for a third on the far side of the field, taking you onto the access road of the white house to your left. Cross this and go

through another tiny stile and wicket gate. Cross the next field, aiming slightly left to intersect the access road. Now follow the right-hand edge of the field, aiming for a stile in the wall corner on the right. Squeeze through this and continue with a wall on your left in front of the farmhouse and crossing a beck by a little bridge. Climb to the stile and head diagonally up the bank on your left to a gate into the farmyard of **Hall Bank**.

Walk straight ahead between the barns and pass through a stile. Now follow the wall on your right as it drops to another stile. Cross a ditch and turn left up a farm track in front of the buildings of **Well Head**. Walk along the top of the field with a wall on your left to a gate. Cross the next field to a gate joining an enclosed track. Walk down to the double gate, turning left in front of a row of converted farm buildings and crossing a bridge. Go straight ahead over an old lane and join an enclosed path to a gate. Walk out onto the surfaced track and descend right. Turn left to walk in front of **East Backstonegill**. In front of a pair of gates, an arrow points you left up a bank to a tiny gate into a field. Turn right along the field edge. Near the far end, dip right through a gate then go left (note the OS map shows a different route here) to cross a stile into a narrow path. Emerge through a stile and over a single slab bridge and head for the stile opposite. Contour across the next field to another stile and the next by the massive stump of a felled tree. Keep to the right below the next building, crossing a ladder stile at the far end of the barn. Keep the wall and fence on your right and walk round the back of the next buildings, picking out a stone stile in the enclosure beyond.

Aim half left towards **Peggleswright**. Cross the stile to join its access road, but turn off left at the bend to continue down to the next building. At the far end, turn left through a gate and ascend slightly to the left across the field, heading for a gap at the top of the wall on the far side. Follow the hedgerow on the right and walk behind the building then descend to a gate beyond the oil tanks. Turn right and go down the track to the road.

Turn right for 400 yards, then left at a signpost for **Cross House Lane**. Go through a gate at the end of the

barn and follow the left-hand field edge down to a gate. Continue to **Tommy Bridge** and, across the bridge, pick up the signs for the **Dales Way**. Follow them right, along the riverside path, then left, over a hillock, with waymarkers keeping you on the line. The path descends to a ladder stile onto a road.

Cage Farm, just along the road here, was once one of four knitting schools in the dale. In the 18th century, hand-knitting provided a vital secondary source of income to many families and the Dentdale folk (men, women and children knitted) acquired a national reputation for their fearsomely quick fingers as the 'terrible knitters of Dent'.

Cross the road and then a bridge and turn right, signposted 'Church Bridge'. Follow the beckside path until it reaches the **River Dee**. Now follow the river until the path kinks away to cross **Keld Beck**. Pass the football pitch and emerge on the road by the bridge. Turn left back into the village, keeping on up the main street to pass the **Sedgwick memorial.**

20 Arnside Knott and Tower

Arnside Tower, a medieval pele tower

Distance 4$^1/_2$ miles 🕐 2$^1/_2$ hours
Map: OS Explorer OL7 (GR 454786)

How to get there

From junction 36 on the M6, head briefly east on the A590, taking the first exit at the next roundabout to go north on the A65. In $^1/_2$ mile turn left on the B6385 to Milnthorpe. In the centre of the town go straight ahead at the crossroads and continue on the B5282, reaching Arnside in 3$^1/_2$ miles. After passing under the railway bear right into the centre of the village. **Parking:** There is free, on-street parking along the promenade opposite the Albion pub.

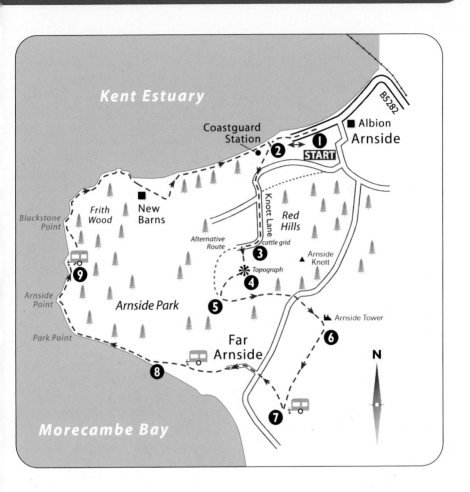

Introduction

Cumbria is not usually associated with the seaside, and yet the county boasts over 100 miles of coastline. This walk explores probably its most interesting section – the remote woodland and rocky inlets that ring the limestone mound of Arnside Knott. The route avoids the actual summit of the Knott – a disappointingly overgrown affair, though completists may wish to add the necessary half mile. Instead it passes over the shoulder of the hill, taking in a panoramic view of the Kent estuary and the Lakeland hills beyond. The journey back is through windblown woods by the low cliff edge. This is as different in character when the tide is in from that at low tide to make it worth doing the walk again on another day.

Drive and Stroll

The Albion

One of a pair of Thwaites' pubs in the village, the Albion is prominently sited above the main road junction on Arnside's promenade. It's a good place for sandwiches and light bites during the day or something a bit more substantial at any time. Think of chicken stacks, pork towers, wedges and nachos and you'll catch the flavour of the menu. Telephone: 01524 761226.

THE WALK

①

Follow the promenade to the road end and bear right to **New Barns** around **Ashmeadow House**. The walkway leads round the corner to the coastguard station.

The dilapidated building here was once a boatyard.

 ②

Just before this, turn left, up the bank past the **Beach Walk café**. Walk up the path to a road and turn right. As it dips down, ignore footpaths to the left and right, then turn left on a lane, signposted to the Knott. Walk up the hill then round a bend to cross a cattle grid.

  ③

About 100 yards on, several paths lead steeply up to the left. They converge at a topograph, overlooking the **Kent valley**. If you don't fancy the climb, you can

continue along this bridleway from the end of the car park through a series of gates in the woodland, to rejoin the main route further on at point 5.

Peak baggers may wish to locate the summit of the Knott (at 521 ft it is the lowest 'Marilyn' in England – this means it is bottom of a list of summits, the term is meant to be a humorous addition to Munro's table of Scottish 3,000 footers). From here, it's about 400 yards away up the hill beyond a wall and some trees, but the view is no better and from the trig point itself is largely obscured by trees. The Knott itself is made of limestone and has become an important site for butterflies, with 34 species now identified.

 ④

From the topograph, facing the slope, turn right downhill, on a path close to the wall. Shortly, beyond some low-hanging trees, you'll see a tiny gate. Go through this and follow the path beyond to a junction by a pair of benches. Maintain your direction to join a descending path leading to a gate and a fingerpost.

Arnside

This is the point where those who chose the lower route rejoin. Take the left-hand gate on the bridleway to **Arnside Tower**. Descend to the road and cross over, heading down the access road opposite towards the farm. Bear right in the farmyard, emerging through a gate at the end of the white building. Pick the centre path here, rising up the bank below the tower to pass to its right.

The tower is one of several pele towers built in the 15th century to defend travellers on the sands route across the bay. It's unusual for being freestanding – not attached to subsequent farm buildings. It was badly damaged by fire in 1602 and much of the interior was removed in the 1680s. To compound the sorry tale, a storm in 1884 caused part of the south-west wall to collapse. It is not open to the public.

Drive and Stroll

Turn right through a gate to an enclosed path signposted to Silverdale via Cove Road. You emerge in a holiday park. Keep to the lower road and after 300 yards turn right by a dog waste bin.

Leave the park through a gate and cross the field beyond. Follow the left edge of the next field to emerge onto a road. Cross over to join the road for **Far Arnside** and continue on into the holiday park. Maintain your direction amongst the caravans, choosing the middle route to **White Creek**. Bear left at the sign for **Knott Drive** and as the road hairpins, keep on under yew trees into the wood.

Pass a broken-down wall and bear left. Now follow the obvious path around the edge of **Park Point**. Through a narrow gateway the path continues round **Arnside Point** and eventually sweeps inland to round the head of a bay. Bear left through the wall by a caravan, then duck through a gap in the scrub on your left to join the foreshore.

The tides race in across the sands here and there's even a bore (a tidal wave) up the channel of the River Kent. There used to be a bell on the chimney of the Albion pub warning of the tide's approach. Now a siren sounds in the summer months (a new automated siren came into operation at the coastguard station in 2007).

Continue around the craggy fingers of **Blackstone Point** on the far side, picking up the path once more. As you approach the bay at **New Barns**, keep to the footpath past cottages and, at the end of the seawall, turn left and keep on the foreshore all the way back into **Arnside**.